The People

Sunderland
A River of Life

by

Jack Curtis

This photograph was taken in the old railway marshalling yards and engine sheds opposite St John's Church and School in Prospect Row. My Uncle Tom Scott is on the right of the four men. Ralph Annison was the shed foreman and would let me into the sheds if there was a new Pacific class locomotive being serviced – exciting stuff in those far off days.

Copyright © Jack Curtis 2003

First published in 2003 by

The People's History Ltd
Suite 1
Byron House
Seaham Grange Business Park
Seaham
Co. Durham
SR7 0PY

ISBN 1 902527 38 0

Contents

Dedicated to

A young fighter pilot of World War Two

A young merchant seaman of World War Two

A very old diver of unforgettable memory

Acknowledgements

The rise of Sunderland from a 16th century tiny fishing village to become the most important port between the Humber and the Firth of Forth has always impressed me. The skill and foresight of our early ancestors transformed a silted up shallow river, with a very dangerous entrance, into a port which could handle between 5,000 and 7,000 sailing ships a year by the late 18th century. It is a story of brilliance and determination for the benefit of all who have lived here. My task in telling this story has been made easier by access to the following:

Reports from Sir John Rennie, Member of the Institution of Civil Engineers, dated 1822 and 1831, etc, with pier specifications included. Plus his 'The Theory Formation and Construction of British and Foreign Harbours' of 1854.

A copy of the 1886 Specification and Engineering drawing of the 50 ton radial block-setting crane, and pier details designed by Henry H. Wake MICE for the construction of the main outer piers built at the turn of the 20th century.

A full transcript of the design and creation of the Hudson Dock, opened in 1850 and published by the Sunderland Post Limited of West Wear Street in 1900: complete with maps of the river mouth and port in the years 1700, 1750, 1800, 1850 and 1900.

The Burleigh & Thompson map of the River Wear from the New Bridge at Chester-le-Street to the Bar at the river mouth dated 1737.

A copy of the *Sunderland Echo* dated the 10th October 1934, commemorating the opening of the Corporation Quay, which provided a magnificent deep water facility for the port.

To both Harry Ramshaw and Ken Harriman for their insights into underground workings of deep offshore coal mines, also Stuart Miller for his 'Life of John Murray' giving an insight into the personality and genius of this truly great man to whom we all owe a great deal indeed.

My late and unforgettable maternal grandfather, who's home and work took me into the very heart of our port before I could even walk. This gave me an insight into heavy industry and a 'university' education free of charge. Thanks also to my wife, Margaret, for her proof reading.

I must also acknowledge the ordinary but – in my opinion – extraordinary men who, dressed in hob nailed boots, cloth caps, woollen mufflers, with hands covered in calluses, tramped the streets of Sunderland day in and day out, working in shipyards, mines, foundries, forges and railways. And, of course, the men in 'white collars' who ran our industry and helped raise Sunderland to the very pinnacle of international fame.

Plus the many people who have helped with photographs, in particular: Ian S. Carr, Brian Holden, George Nairn, Alan Tedder, the Sunderland Echo and Sunderland Port Authority.

Jack Curtis

Generations of A River of Life

This photograph shows River Wear Commissioners' diver, Ralph Scott – the author's grandfather – carrying out routine maintenance work on the hard limestone fabric of the Number One Gateway which was the main entrance to the South Dock. This picture pre-dates the building of the Corporation Quay of 1934. This is proven by looking above the aft end of the nearest tug which shows the old look out complete with signal flagstaff. This formed part of what is known as the promenade at the north east corner of the old Barracks. The two tugs were owned by Lambton, Hetton & Joicey Coal Company as distinguished by the three red bands on their black funnels. They towed the colliers from Lambton Coal Staithes which were up above the town bridges and opposite the Sheepfolds. One of these two could be *Eppleton Hall*, which crossed the Atlantic, to form part of a museum in San Francisco. J.L. Thompson's Shipyard forms the back drop to the whole scene.

The year 2000 saw Jonathon
Punshon – the author's grandson
– visit the home ground of his
great-great-grandparents, Ralph
and Sushannah Scott. They lived
on these very docks for almost
thirty years. The diving punt for
calm water work was always
moored below this quay, which
is adjacent to the old Gladstone
Bridge in the half tide basin.

Ralph Scott rising from the
watery depths just outside the
dock entrance to place those
great heavy lead-soled boots
upon the iron rungs of the
ascent ladder. This diving suit
can be seen today in Sunderland
Museum.

This photograph of the author (right), as Contracts Engineer, with Eric Lee, the Supplies Engineer of NEEB, was taken under the stern end of an SD 14 ship while rewiring the electrical welding ring mains around the berth. It shows the slipway running down the beach, propeller boss and welded joints to perfection, with the old break water running out into the North Sea, which shows Bartram's did launch direct into the sea. The only UK shipyard to do so.

BORN ON THE NORTH MOOR

The way we were at Moor Board School
in 1936, with Harry Miller, front, then
myself (left) and Freddie Lincoln, with
Annie Appleby on the left, one of the
Blenkinsop girls, while the other name
escapes me, but no offence meant.

I was born in October of 1930 in North Moor Street – built on the old north end of the Moor. This was the year that also saw my first home being demolished to allow the Corporation Quay to be built. My ancestors have served Sunderland in many guises: fishermen, river pilots, marine engineers, shipbuilders, housebuilders and diver – right back to as far as at least 1729. They saw and lived through all of this recorded history and would that I could sit and talk to them all to apply more flesh to the bones of the men who made it all possible for so many dependant people. Living in the Barracks as a boy enabled me to see and indeed remember most of the old East End before it was swept away in the great slum clearances which ripped the heart out of old Sunderland; removing forever the many old familiar landmarks and homes of our ancestors. We ran around the whole area, playing deligo before the Garths were built and the wartime blackout came; seeing most of the old streets illuminated by wall mounted gas lights. High Street East was a mass of side alleys running off to right and left with most of them running down to either the river or Low Street. This was once the centre of trade in the old town but in my time was full of bonded warehouses. Portland Blue Circle Cement came by the shipload to Wylam Wharf with the ferry landing between it and the Brewery which stood just west of the Fish Quay. Austin's Bank ran west passing Duke's furniture factory which stood opposite the Scotia Engine Works. At the seaward end stood George Pott's old Tagarine Shop, a row of garages and then the sailmakers premises with its old fashioned hoist bracket protruding out from above the top floor door. Then there was the Mortuary (or Deed House as it was called) along towards the old Custom House.

A lovely photograph of the old Hendon outlet to the docks with the lifeboat hitting the water after running down the slipway. The cobles and tugs give a good guide as to how things were, with the old wood piles standing stark against the water as it shimmers in the background.

In earlier years Low Street held many public houses and quite a few premises of ill repute, plus gin kitchens which catered for all levels of society. This was a scene that could be encountered in any sea port such as ours with ships coming and going by the dozen with every tide, plus the keelmen coming and going back and forth with load after load of coal from the inland pits of that time. Today in the year 2003 the East End of my boyhood has all but vanished, however there are a couple of spots from which I can review an area which was once my world way back in the 1930s, '40s and '50s in a Sunderland vastly different to the one I live in today. Growing up in the old East End gives one a ready feel for the place. I can see most of the old streets in my mind's eye so let me take you down to the Welcome Tavern and stand at its main door looking west along what was Prospect Row. Our view along the old engine wall to our left shows shadows from the past in the shape of bricked-up doorways and windows that were houses way back. First there is the briefest outline of the Williams' house. Further west lived the McGoughs, and, nearest the gates, Stan Close and his family lived. But today they are just shadowy memories on the old engine wall.

Opposite these houses stood both the church and school of St John's and beyond these, on the corner of Moorgate Street, stood Tommy Hutchinson's pub, the Station Hotel. Here Johnny Cochrane, the

Here is a photograph of a charabanc trip, probably away from Tommy Hutchy's pub, the Station Hotel in Prospect Row, in the 1930s. Note the vehicle itself, a real open-topped charabanc if ever there was one. I only recognise two men: my grandfather, Ralph Scott, on the right with hand in pocket and Walter McGough, in white shirt with no tie on.

Bobby Gurney (standing) sees his header hit the back of the net during the 1937 FA Cup Final. One of Sunderland's other goalscorers that day was Hendon-born Raich Carter (lying on the ground). Sunderland beat Preston North End 3-1 to win the FA Cup for the first time in the club's history.

manager of Sunderland AFC, signed many of his star players to create the 1930s side which won the FA Cup and also the First Division Championship. The great thing about these two major milestones in the club's history is that Horatio Stratton Carter was the captain of the team, and Raich, as he was known, was a Sunderland man born and bred. His father played for Sunderland Royal Rovers when my grandfather captained that team which played along the Lonnen at Hendon where Brian Mills stands now. Carter Senior later signed as a professional for Southampton, while the Royal Rovers created the record of winning of the Shipowners' Cup, Monkwearmouth Charity Cup and the Wearside League Cup all in one season. They were the first team to win the Shipowners' Cup when it was put up for competition.

Turning back to the door of the Welcome Tavern and this time looking north, I can visualise the length of Barrack Street just as it was when I was a boy. The Moor Board School was behind the houses on the left hand side, with access to the school from Stafford Street for the boys and Chapel Street for the infants and girls. Quite a few old boys were killed in the Second World War. They were lads older than me but lads I knew quite well, including my cousin who carried the same name as myself. He was torpedoed in mid-Atlantic on the 5th May 1943, aged 23 years, when a pack of 34 U-Boats waited for his convoy. It was one of the last Wolf Pack attacks of the war which devastated that particular convoy.

Austin Scott, who lived just out our back, was a motorcycle fanatic and from one the great foyboat families of Wearside. He also never came back from the war; while Roger Weston was killed in Bomber Command. It was widely believed that Roger would have had a brilliant football career at the highest level.

This magnificent photograph of the Royal Rovers football team was taken at the end of the 1900-01 season when this brilliant local side created a record which was not equalled until the 1960s. They won the three splendid trophies displayed here. The superb Shipowners' Cup is on the left, the Monkwearmouth Charity Cup on the right and the Wearside League Championship Cup in the centre. The committee and trainers who ran the team are the twelve stalwart men in suits and collars and ties. Bill Lazenby is on the left and was the main driving force and secretary of the team. The team were, back row: E. Lowes, George Souter, Bob Wood. Middle row: Ralph Scott (captain), Tommy Stewart, T. Shipley, Sammy Curle, Jimmy Hannah (Scottish international who played for Sunderland's 'Team of All the Talents'), J. Wood. Front row: W.S. Taylor, George Harvey, Billy Berry, T. Brown and G.H. Gidley. There must be many hundreds of people on Wearside today who are descended from these brilliant footballers of yesteryear. All of the players signed professional forms at some time in their careers. They were a wonderful team which deserves to be remembered for winning the Wearside League four times, the Shipowners' Cup three times and the Monkwearmouth Charity Cup three times – and all within a five-year period.

Another local lad was Jimmy Taylor who lies in a grave in Jakarta out in Java. Having survived the war in Europe he went to fight the Japanese, after having won the DFC as a pilot with Coastal Command, flying first Beaufighters and later Mosquitos. He was a real boyhood hero of mine and in truth still is even after I have passed my three score years and ten. There could well have been others who paid the full price of war, however their omission is due to ignorance, not intent, and would that I could name them all for their's was true valour in our darkest hours. These are the thoughts which come from standing at the Welcome Tavern. My thoughts are also for the many other people I knew, for the old East End that I loved was made up of people rather than the buildings which housed them.

In my day the Barracks wall ran north from the Welcome Tavern to the south entrance gate, with its imposing stone pillars, but minus its gates. Only one block of the original three remained, the other two were demolished for the construction of the new dock entrance, built when the old North Moor Street entrance was lost due to the building of the Corporation Quay. I wired this block for electricity in 1954.

A group of residents of the old Barracks in the East End, all now long since passed away, but fine women with a zest for life. They knew what a poss tub was for and never needed aerobics to keep themselves fit and in shape. The lady lying at the front is Alice Crawford; while on her right sits Bella Kell; extreme left front, in stripes, is Nellie Maddison; next to her in her Tam is my mother, Ethel Curtis; then Mrs Reay; Ginny Bailey; with Pansy Reay with her hand on Bella's shoulder. My Aunt Belle, also in her Tam, is behind Nellie; then Meggie Mitchinson above Mrs Reay and Pop Mitchinson above her. Last but not least is Ginny Simmonds while the boy and the other two lady's names escape me. The girl on the far right is Joan Crawford when she was about ten years old.

A pre-war photograph taken outside the Bungalows in Barrack Street. I recognise Jenny and Annie Jobling at each end of the back row. Ruth Crawford is centre back; one of the Buckle girls has the ribbon in her hair; Florence Reay with the wide smile and Liz Mitchinson centre front. These houses were built to take people dislodged by the building of the Corporation Quay, said to be a five-year short term move. I was six months old when we moved in and over forty years old before my mother moved out and they were demolished.

I remember the construction in great detail, even to the smell of pitch pine as I drilled the king beams to allow the cables to pass through them. Knowing all of the families that lived there made it a very pleasant job to do. The old well shaft lined with stone was partially hidden in the scarping of the bankside of the dock access road. It must still be there, hidden from sight and is the only old well I have ever come across in the whole area, a rare legacy indeed and reminder of days long past. The roof trusses and purlins of the old Barracks were all hand cut, sawn square on three sides only and axe trimmed on the fourth. The joints were all either half lapped or mortice and tenon, secured with wooden dowels. I noticed that the floor boards were all plain with no sign of tongue and groove as in later floors I lifted, while the nails were all hand cut and as good as new. These were the little things you noticed on old buildings. By taking the new entrance road through the north gates of the Barracks they ripped the guts out of the place; and removed much of the old drill square for the angled road to sweep down towards the granaries. Along with the north and south blocks, when viewed correctly it shows how massive the complex was, with magazines to store ammunition, volleyball courts, and all of the other peripheral building associated with military establishments.

Walking west from the present dock entrance, our first meeting with the past would be the Boars Head pub, now sadly closed and looking for a new tenant or owner, but I wouldn't hold my breath for success in that area. On again we come to the Clarendon once owned by Tommy and Billy Carr, with the Davison family running the pub when I was a boy. Then one of the original alleys is found next to the old pub named Bull Lane. It has linked High Street East to the Lower Quay for centuries and literally thousands of old East Enders must have used it for access. Dicky Wilkinson's funeral parlour is now a newsagents and general dealer. These are the most easterly remnants of the old town existing today apart from the 1934 wall of the Corporation Quay, which really doesn't qualify as being old. Moving on along High Street East the next surviving relics are just beyond the bottom of Church Street where we find the deplorable neglected property which housed Grater's pork shop. Next door is or was Joe Hall's butchers shop, then Snowball's general dealers and Rutherford's the shipping butcher at the corner of James William Street. My mother dealt with Joe Hall for many years while we would buy savaloys from Grater's after we had been to the Gaiety Cinema to see Tom Mix or the Cisco Kid or serials like *The Mummy's Hand* or *Flash Gordon* at the Penny Matinee. I can see the half pigs hanging from the great row of steel hooks in Grater's shop now, with fresh sawdust spread beneath them to absorb any blood dripping from them. Harry, Louey and Mrs Grater served behind the counter and much delicious food was to be obtained, such as a 'Duck with a veil on' and things of that type.

The old derelict Orphanage on the edge of the Town Moor is a drab sight today but wasn't always so when used for its true purpose of housing and training sons of sea-going men who had lost their lives. This group photograph was taken around 1911, showing Mr King and his daughter on the left, other staff on the right and twenty-three boys including my father second right, second row from the back, all displayed in their traditional naval dress.

Turning back to Church Street, and walking up towards the south, there are just a couple of old renovated properties still in existence. The church still dominates our view and this is the Sunderland Parish Church of the Holy Trinity, to give it its correct title. It has played a significant part in the lives of many of my ancestors as well as myself and hopefully, if common sense prevails, it will survive into the future because of its special place in the history of Sunderland. We go there occasionally to a service. However, Trafalgar Square is still standing with Nelson's battle signal emblazoned along the centre soffitt, a fitting tribute to our greatest admiral, and home to many old sailors.

Just east of the church is the Donnison School which predates all of the Board Schools. It was run as a fee paying school before the Education Acts were passed which produced such a great rise in the literacy of Sunderland's many children. The old Orphanage is still standing, but only just, with boarded windows it looks totally dejected. My father spent several years within its precincts.

That short mental walk just about covers the total historical remains of the original town of Sunderland. The really old town has vanished without trace: Fishers Row; the Rope Walk; the Hat Case; the Barracks; Warren Street built over the rabbit or coney warrens; the Pottery

Just after the Second World War, the Sunderland Sea Cadets made their HQ in the old Pottery buildings, which can just be seen above the bus. They were often drilled along Barrack Street in the evening as this photograph shows. The wall behind them is part of the original Barracks, as is the roof of the building behind. The bus shows the sign for Dock Circle which meant it ran around the East End via Fawcett Street in a loose circular run. Most of these lads will be drawing their old age pension now but they must make you feel proud by their look of sheer dedication to duty.

Building which was the meeting place of the town's Quaker community; and High Street Wesleyan Chapel which I attended as a boy. I wonder how many remember the Ice House between the Boars Head and the Clarendon, Stamp Lane, Golden Alley, Fighting Cock Alley, Bull Lane and the Mill Hill where apparently the May Day celebrations were held around the Maypole. I can remember the old Gray School on the edge of the Moor and going there on winter evenings during the war when it became the Gray Boys' Club. This brings another link into my East End chain, as both of my grandfathers attended this school around the years 1880 to 1890, but it too, like almost everything else, has vanished.

The East End of my boyhood days in the 1930s and '40s brings people like the Valente sisters to mind. Their family kept the ice cream shop opposite the Orphanage and the sisters would wheel their barrow around the area, selling cornets and sandwiches to anyone who could afford them. Our dustbins were emptied into horse-drawn dust carts. It was quite common to see children giving the horse bread crusts, provided the wind was right and you did not get covered with dust as coal fires produced a lot of ash.

We had a big black iron fire and oven combined in the living room. It was the only fire in the house and it heated a back boiler into the bargain. It was very cost effective when you consider it with heating, cooking and hot water all from that one fire. In very cold winter weather we were given an oven shelf wrapped in a blanket to put in the bed. That was sheer luxury, but it had to be really cold, with the bedroom windows all patterned with ferns and lace when you woke up the next morning.

Moor Board School infants class drinking milk in the school yard in 1935. Left to right: Conrad Culkin, myself, Bernie McCue, Fred Lincoln, Jimmy Urch and Billy Corner. We even had flowers on the table.

Moor Board School football team, 1932-33 season – winners of the Councillor Pickering Cup. Back row: Jimmy Cheal (from Prospect Row), George Crow (Harrison's Buildings), Eddie Neal (Vine Street), Billy Taylor (Stafford Street) George Watt (Burleigh Street), Gordon Scott (The Barracks). Middle row: Mr Charles Benson (Headmaster), Ralph Crawford (The Barracks), George Johnson (Harrison's Buildings), Jimmy Taylor (The Barracks), Roger Weston (Thomas Street), Mr Arthur Herdman. Front, sitting: Jackie Ellis (North Moor Street) with the ball at his feet and Billy Wickham with the all important date details.

Only one player in this photograph had proper football boots and he was Jimmy Taylor. The rest played in whatever they could get their hands on, while the ball itself was obtained through all of the school saving OXO coupons and sending for it when they had sufficient. A far cry from today! I know that both Jimmy Taylor and Roger Weston played for Hylton Colliery Juniors when they were the top junior team in the area. Jimmy signed for Newcastle United but the war put a stop to that. This is a lovely photograph, taken in the old school yard, of lads who had grown up in the hard Depression of the hungry 1920s and '30s.

One of the many trips away from High Street East Wesleyan Chapel some time in the 1960s. Many East Enders would come together for these enjoyable excursions, such as this one to Northern Ireland. Sadly they are all long gone but their descendents will remember the pleasure they gained through these social trips, with the singing and dancing which followed wherever they went.

My great-grandmother, Isabella Earl, standing in High Street East, well over 100 years ago.

This strikingly dressed young woman is believed to be Catherine Bowey probably playing Mary Queen of Scots in a play put on at High Street Wesleyan Chapel, somewhere around 1915. Catherine lived in Moorgate Street and certainly looked the part with her beautiful ruff and string of pearls.

This is Alderman Jack Oxley from Hendon, who for many years was the senior Labour Alderman on Sunderland Council and never received any payments for his service. He is photographed with his niece, Joan.

We made slides across the Moor Board School yard when it froze and would queue up to take turns to run up then slide across the yard. Other times we would play knocky out with white pot tossies, spending the whole playtime at this game, ending up with bulging pockets if you had your eye in. Cricket was also played in the yard during the summer when Mr Patterson the headmaster would invariably join in to show his skills off to us lads. At other times we were taken by bus and then tram up to Sparks Farm to play football on the many pitches there.

Those were halcyon days when it never seemed to rain. The women of the Barracks would get their heads together during the school holidays and organise a day out to Roker. Off we would all troop, and by all I mean everyone in the Barracks, off up Warren Street then High Street East, finally ending up at the ferry. Fare one half penny and over to Monkwearmouth we went. We all trudged along past J.L. Thompson's Shipyard, past the North Dock, then down past Armstrong Addison's the timber preservers to end up between the piers on the sands where we would spend the entire day. Golden sands, beautiful sunshine, table cloths spread with rocks placed on the corners, egg sandwiches, banana sandwiches, cakes and cans of tea scalded up at the bank top. Then swimming or searching for crabs amongst the rocks, playing games and building sand castles. It was all mothers and children because in those days our fathers were at work from 7.30 am to 5.00 pm. Most of our mothers did not work and believe me they gave us some great times to remember. Money never entered into it.

My mother, Ethel Curtis (née Scott), with some of her swimming pupils taken on the beach between the piers around 1938. We all went here from the Barracks for the full day, almost like an army on the march. I see Liz Mitchinson on my mother's left, Florence Reay on her right and Ruth Crawford behind her, with the other girl being Isabelle Jobling. I make up the group.

LIGHTHOUSE, ROKER.

The drum head and lighthouse around 1905, with our ancestors taking a bracing stroll along this wonderful new pier which carried you almost a mile out to sea.

A very old view of Seaburn tram terminus with the gas light being cleaned while the cleaner's bike is leaning against the lighting column. The whole roadway shows cobble stone paving as its best, while the tram stands ready for its journey to the town centre.

Money was tight but you got your Saturday penny, anything else had to be earned. So if the gang wanted to see a special picture like *The Adventures of Robin Hood* we got a barrow that one of us had made and went down to the East Coast Timber Company at the bottom of the dock bank. We bought threepenny worth of slatts cut from the sides of pit props, brought them up and then cut them into eight inch pieces. We chopped them up into sticks and tied them up with string. Then we went round the streets selling them to raise enough cash to get the whole gang a seat in the Gods at the Palace Cinema near the Londonderry pub on Crowtree Road. We ran there and ran back because it would have cost another penny each for bus fare, which was well beyond our means. I can still see the shadow of Errol Flynn and Basil Rathbone fencing on the stairs of Nottingham Castle. That film brought on a great rash of sword fights amongst us all. Our neighbour, Mr Reay who was a carpenter, made me a beautiful sword with finger guard. I felt invincible when I got carried away with the spirit of the Green Wood. Bows and arrows too played their part, usually made from the bamboo rods from the house curtains when our mother wasn't looking, but it cost you a sore backside.

Every time I go to the MetroCentre at Gateshead I am reminded of the old Market which stretched from High Street up to Coronation Street with an entrance at each end. For it was to me the MetroCentre

This is the cast of one of the High Street Chapel's popular shows which they put on at regular intervals. Included in the back row are: Auntie Belle, extreme right; Meggie Maughan next to her; Auntie Susie, fifth from the right; Annie Smart, extreme left; with Ralph Gowland, all in white next to her. Ralph's wife, with the flower in her hair, is kneeling in front of him. Ned Thompson is on her right with Pastor Ford and my cousin Isabelle in front of them. All good clean enjoyment amongst very nice people.

of its day, even down to having its own fair ground at the south end near Coronation Street. I remember going through it quite a few times before the Second World War. It was packed full of people until very late on with stalls selling everything under the sun – Veiti's hardware and haberdashery, Joe the Bacon Man, Franklin's sweet stall, second-hand clothes, second-hand furniture, groceries, crockery, meat – it was all there. The bottom entrance came out beside the Coffee Pot Shop run by the Chapman family and opposite, next to Bradbury the Undertaker, was the Herbalist Store. They made and sold the most superb Sarsaparilla I have ever tasted in my entire life. We used to go there every Saturday night, that is my father, mother and me, after we came out of the Market. Boy did I look forward to that visit. There were great polished oak casks on tresils against the back wall, wooden taps fitted into the hole at the bottom and a mountain of froth on the top of your glass.

The East End was bustling with life even though times were hard. I can remember the dole queue in Symrna Place with men standing four deep and running back two or three hundred yards. My parents received one shilling per week (five pence in today's money) to keep me if my father was out of work. We could and did raise the money to buy all-day-tickets at four and a half old pence each for children. These allowed you to travel anywhere on either the bus or tramcar for a full day. We toured the town from head to toe, taking in the sights of

Some of the Scott family with a couple of friends standing outside the Dock Master's House on the South Docks' man-made land. This was our spiritual home for many years and gave my ancestors and myself many happy memories. I am standing with head bowed at the front, aged three years.

Sunderland from the upper deck. Easily affordable half penny 'progs' were available in most sweet shops. These were when you could win a prize by pricking (or proging) a small box with a target on the front and removing a paper caption telling you what you had won. A Silver Link Toffee was the lowest prize and maybe a pocket knife for a top prize, with other things in between. I particularly liked and enjoyed the home-made ginger beer our mother made for us and can still feel the tickle in the nose it gave you and the peppery taste afterwards. It was all made with pure ingredients – delicious!

There were many relics from the past still in existence in my boyhood. There was the Band Stand on the Moor with a massive concrete square and wooden forms around its edges, where open air dances and concerts had taken place in earlier years. Octagon Cottage at Ray's Landsale with its unique architecture should have been preserved and maintained in perpetuity. It stood at the top of Extension Road which led down to the south end of the docks. There was also of course the very old retired seamen's homes known as the Assembly Garth which was opposite the old original cemetery and adjacent to the Parish Church. The old 'Kitty' or jail was still there at the bottom of Coronation Street, opposite the south entrance of the old Market built in 1828. These were all demolished without thought to either the past, present or future, as was our magnificent Town Hall in Fawcett Street. While the modern additions have much to commend them, they lack the essential flavour of by gone eras, as does the Civic Centre and other additions.

This view of Fawcett Street shows to perfection our magnificent Town Hall as it stood there in our glory days of world shipbuilding domination and when five million tons of coal was exported every year.

A closer view of the Town Hall from the early 1900s. Note the flags are flying at half mast. Also in the picture are: an open-top tramcar, a large flat four wheel cart and heavy horse, a wood tower barrow and what looks like an ice cream cart. I worked from a tower barrow identical to this one when I installed the first sodium lighting along Newcastle Road after the end of the Second World War.

Binns Store on the east side of Fawcett Street. It was altered and adapted many times before being burned down by incendiary bombs during the last war.

Our town in the 1940s and '50s saw a massive influx of miners and their families every Saturday. We had seen them come for many many years as Sunderland was a real shopping metropolis for them, with a massive range of department stores full of top quality merchandise to suit everyone's pocket. We had Kennedy's Cobden Exchange at the top of High Street West near the junction with Crowtree Road; Blackett's opposite the taxi rank at the north end of the Railway Station in Union Street; and Joplings store opposite West Sunniside and Norfolk Street. Their first store was at the bottom of High Street Bank, almost opposite the Golden Lion public house. There was also of course Binns Store, who's name was embellished on every bus and tram with the slogan 'Shop at Binns For Everything'. People obtained credit from the club man or club woman who loaned money at set interest rates over a fixed period of time. They either called at your home every week or you could pay men like Mr Martin who sat in Blackett's every Saturday collecting cash from miners or shipyard workers who queued up to pay their fixed weekly amounts. The working classes furnished their homes through getting a 'club off' and bought new radios, washing machines and many other items to improve their lives. The Co-op Store ran a massive dividend scheme where for every pound spent in their store the customer was allocated 2s 6d into their account. It could be redeemed for goods or as cash if you so desired that. It was often allowed to run on for special events such as a wedding or to pay for a funeral.

The opening of the electric tramway system in Sunderland on 15th August 1900. Note the smart civic dignitaries – with silk top hats or bowlers – and the garlands of flowers around the upper deck of the trams with the elaborate cast iron lamp standard in the foreground.

The transport system was a mixture of buses and trams which were very efficient and run with exact timetables that were strictly adhered to. In the 1950s our shipyards had full order books worth many millions of pounds and the mines were working full tilt. National Service awaited all of us who were physically fit, once we reached 18 or 21 years of age. It gave most of us two years of great experience and took us abroad for the very first time in our lives, if we were lucky enough to get an overseas posting. Britain was still a world power in those days. Generation gaps did not exist in my youth as we apprentices were placed one to one with older, well experienced tradesmen who taught us the practical skills of our various trades. I worked with artists of the electrical installation techniques, men who you learned to respect and admire even though they only wore navy blue boilersuits. I genuinely feel sorry for the youth of today who will never have these types of traditional benefits which was the British way of training our workforce. We trooped to evening classes at the Tech, or to be correct Sunderland Technical College in Green Terrace, in our thousands, three nights a week and always after a full day's work from 7.30 am until 5.20 pm. It was tough but very beneficial to both ourselves and Sunderland.

My working world in the electrical installation industry took me into virtually every other industry or commercial business and of course the domestic field. No one can have had a broader spectrum of experience than I was fortunate enough to have. I have experienced Sunderland from many different angles, such as the: deck of a tugboat; the floodlight towers of Roker Park Football Ground; culverts under the East Quay of the docks; crane cabins on the Corporation Quay; the top of Roker Lighthouse; the service ducts under the Royal Hospital; the Bright Beer Plant at the old Vaux Brewery and many other places. I know Sunderland and love Sunderland, as my ancestors have for many generations.

This is me looking seawards at the end of one of Bartram's crane gantries on the completion of electrical ring mains to supply the welding equipment for producing the then world famous SD 14 cargo ships. The cabling and Reyrolle HH Switchgear are visible at the end of the gantry, as is the stern end of the ship under construction. This shows a little of the scope and skills of our labour force. The stern post and frame with the propeller boss were usually manufactured at Wolsingham Steel Works and can be seen shored up ready for welding into place. My grandparent's house stood just opposite the main gates into Bartram's Shipyard and I played on this very beach quite often in the 1930s when the Depression was at its height.

This strange looking vehicle driven by Sam Bagley was an electrically powered van, one of several used over a period of some 40 or so years by firstly the Sunderland Corporation Electricity Undertaking and subsequently by its successor the North Eastern Electricity Board. Based in Dunning Street, its headquarters were eventually incorporated into the Vaux Brewery Complex when NEEB moved its HQ to Penshaw. The SCEU, as the Sunderland Corporation Electricity Undertaking was known, was a brilliant organisation with a very forward looking long term planning attitude which gave Sunderland one of the very best electrical distribution systems in the country. It had its own power station and high voltage distribution network with strategically placed sub-stations which transformed the supply to 230 volts single phase for domestic supplies and 380 volts three phase for industry. The policy was to provide every house with a 0.0225 square inch feeder cable, capable of providing all electrical requirements into the foreseeable future and the truth is that these supplies are still in use today in many areas of Sunderland.

These Wilson electric vehicles were charged up over night via metallic selenium rectifiers using cheap off-peak energy and could, and did, run all day around the town. They had a maximum speed of approximately 35 to 40 miles an hour in the early part of the day. They were environmentally friendly long before the issue was even under consideration, proving just how progressive the SCEU really was. They had electric clocks strategically placed around the town, top quality street lighting and supply feeding the tramcar network which again gave green power on this vast system.

The SCEU purchased these Wilson Vehicles some time in the 1930s, or even the 1920s, and painted blue and cream they were a familiar sight around the town. They even owned a massive tower wagon of the same type to repair street lighting columns which developed faults or required lamps changing. The price of domestic electricity during the war was three units for one old penny and the whole organisation ploughed many thousands of pounds back into the rates fund every year, proving what an efficient system it was.

To end this section of my memories of the town, here is a little poem written in the Sunderland vernacular. It is dedicated to the many old fish wives – including some of my own ancestors – who walked our town selling their wares.

The Fish Wife

Did yuh iver see a fish wife
Wark alang a street
Her basket sitting on her heed
Sh' didn't half luck a treet.

A greet lang lily white apron
Und hand made woolun sharl
Heed held high and luvley step
A sight tu be beheld be arl.

A neck wud muv this way und that
As on her heed the basket rode
Wi ringing cry, a wares sh'd call
With grace sh' carried a heavy load.

Sh' ad a greet big pocket
Reet across a apron white
And inter this sh' put a cash
It used tu why a tun by night.

In rain und wind und snar
Sh' warked the streets arl ower town
Often drarked und hungry
Wi the heels uv a shoos worn down.

When sh' got yam on varry card neets
Sh' wud put the cracket aside the fire
Then sit und drink a cuppa tea
And rest there tuv a hearts desire.

Jack Curtis

A ONCE PEACEFUL RIVER

This view is taken from the old quay at the bottom of High Street, just below where the Fish Quay stands today. An artist is completing his work as *Mercandia VI* leaves for Denmark on 15th May 1990. This was the final member of the Wear-built batch of ferryboats to leave the river. *Mercandia VII*, built at Appledore in Devon, left the Wear on 22nd May 1990. On the far side of the river, below the right hand crane, stood the old steps of the ferry boat landing on the Monkwearmouth side of the river.

I must go down to the sea again, to the call of the running tide,
Is a wild call and a clear call that may not be denied,
And all I ask is a windy day with the white clouds flying,
And the flung spray and the blown spume, and the seagulls crying.

Masefield

The history of Sunderland and the River Wear are so inextricably linked as to be one and the same thing. The former was totally dependant upon the latter hence the title of this history, for the Wear is 'A River of Life' for Sunderland. Yet for all of her life-giving energy, it has taken the combined skills and determination of many good men to bend this small unruly river to their will for the benefit of the inhabitants. If we go back in time a mere four hundred years or so we would find a few fishermen's cottages scattered along the south bank of the river mouth. Also here was a small semi-neglected church sitting on a small knoll on the north bank of the river at Monkwearmouth, plus the trampled remains of what was once the greatest monastery in Christendom. The river at that time would be a multi-channelled, shallow outlet into the North Sea, or German Ocean as it was called. The depth of water would be quite shallow allowing people to ford the river quite easily at low tide.

In the aeons of time, before powered flight allowed man to ascend into the sky, we often tried to use a bird's eye view to illustrate a panoramic picture or make a specific point. To achieve this view of the River Wear, around the year 1600, let us assume we are looking through the eyes of a seagull as it flies from Marsden Rock to the river and then upwards into the hinterland. With the tide out, his beady eyes would scan the cliffs from Souter Point and its rocky beach. Along towards Whitburn he would encounter the massive rocky outcrop which exists to this day and is known as the Whitburn Steel. From this point the cliffs decreased in height as they ran south towards what is now Seaburn, where a little burn drains into the sea. This is the burn that Bede crossed regularly on his journeys to and from the Monastery at Jarrow. St Paul's was built some years after our own St Peter's Church and Monastery, which trained and educated the Venerable Bede. Flying on, our aerial observer would see the cliffs start rising again as they reached Cannon Ball Rocks, near where the Bede Cross now stands. Then there is another great rocky outcrop which stretched right to the river mouth and ran some several hundred yards out into the North Sea. At this point the cliffs turned almost south west to form the north bank of the river. In 1600 this area was dominated by the north rocks. This tidal estuary was in a perfectly natural state with no man-made structures at all on the river mouth. It was full of multi-shaped sandbars and this gaping entrance moved and changed shape in relationship to the actions of both winds and tides.

The magnificent west tower of St Peter's Church, built in 674 AD. In the 7th century, stone was a new material for most buildings and the glass windows were a source of amazement as no building in Britain had ever been glazed before. The church was the creation of Benedict Biscop's. The monastery trained and educated the Venerable Bede, monk of international acclaim. This picture is taken from an illustration from the late 19th century. Ken Lay and myself must be the only two men living now who helped to install electricity into the church for the first time in 1947 – some 1273 years after it was built.

The labyrinth of channels created by nature was to become the greatest single obstacle to shipping in later years, taxing the skill and ingenuity of everyone involved with the emerging port of Sunderland. Low tide exposed a multitude of rocks with little eddies of water running from pool to pool. Amongst these masses of sand banks and small outcrops of half concealed rocks, many types of sea birds search the tide lines for shell fish and small crustaceans. Meanwhile our gull flew leisurely overhead observing a pristine river entrance of the most complex series of shallow channels. With the rising of the tide most of these features would be concealed, making the entrance or exit from

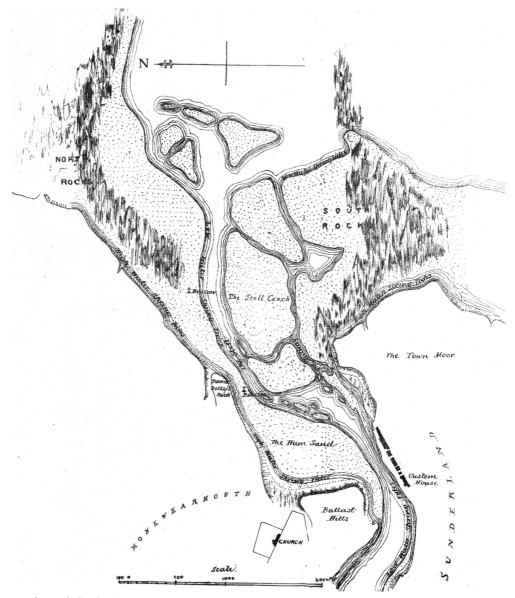

A plan of the harbour at Sunderland from 1700.

the Wear a most difficult and even life-threatening experience for most river travellers of that time. In spring time the tides took the incoming water right up to the base of the cliffs, often causing erosion on a large scale, bringing more debris tumbling into the river mouth. Looking around, our gull would observe equally high cliffs on the south side of the river but these were set back behind the line of the Roker cliffs. Another enormous rocky outcrop ran away south towards what became Hendon and out into the exposed North Sea. This formed a very difficult mouth where any east or south wind could create unbelievable difficulties with only sail and man-power to control ships. The south side cliffs ran almost due west inland, narrowing the river quite dramatically opposite St Peter's Church. The original tiny settlement of cottages on the south bank were due south of the church in an area which must have been very remote and dangerous when the heavy seas ran in unhindered, forcing their way well up stream, scouring the river banks with unremitting force. The angle of a north cliff running south west, then a south cliff running almost due west created a natural funnel into which storm force winds could drive the massive waves, creating havoc in the lower reaches of the river – a harsh environment indeed.

From this gaping mouth the south cliffs turned south east for some 500 yards, then due south to run away past Hendon and on towards Seaham; much as they do today, with the south rocks of soft limestone lying in a great swathe from the cliff bases way out into the North Sea. The basic industry of fishing would create the first real navigators on our river and our flying eye would observe small boats working their way in and out through the shoals and sandbars as they fished the tides. There are no piers or docks in 1600, just a rock encased series of sand bars forming a shallow and treacherous entrance to a very small and difficult river. In truth this seems the most unlikely of rivers to become such a massive player in the Industrial Revolution.

The southern side of the river ran against steep banks and high cliffs which in turn determined the layout of the streets and buildings. This geography produced famous names such as the Long Bank and Pottery Bank, where the legendary Jack Crawford was born. Low Street became the main link to the outside world.

Our eyes in the sky would observe the small humble beginnings of Sunderland through its tiny collection of fishermen's cottages sited about a mile down river from the well and long established village of Bishopwearmouth. The tower and church of St Peter's would stand out like a beacon as the largest building in an area around the river mouth, with many enclosed fields and paddocks on both sides of the river. Flying on inland the north bank would be seen to be much more accessible from the river than the south bank. The southern side was all steep banks and cliffs with great rock faces and stands of timber clothing the whole area. A great rock outcrop some mile or so inland would some 200 years later provide the footings and anchor foundation for our 1796 bridge which was one of the wonders of its age. At that

A very well known photograph of the famous Long Bank, taken in January 1911, gives you a glimpse of our ancestors' world. It is so very different from today as to be almost unrecognisable, yet the people survived and to a large degree prospered.

particular time it was a prototype of immense significance. It was capable of carrying foot passengers, horse-drawn heavy loads, herds of cattle or flocks of sheep. It was a bridge before its time in a sense and without parallel in the North of England. A marvellous and significant development in the creation of a town on both sides of the river, but in the year 1600 not even a dream on our undeveloped and still totally natural river.

Moving on upstream, the valley of the Gill would appear next on the south bank with many signs of man's access to the river from the village of Bishopwearmouth who's people would have used the Wear for several centuries. The curving river swept north west from the Gill, passed the high rising northern bank where the Stadium of Light now stands, which at this period in time in 1600 would be covered in bushes and trees, pre-dating the sinking of Wearmouth Colliery. On the south side, the area of Ayres Quay and then the site of the future Laing's Shipyard would appear, before the river made a turn to the south west. Following this turn our gull would espy the little town of Suddick sitting up on the north bank with a scattering of dwellings and rural industries running down to the river. A narrow country lane ran up from Monkwearmouth which in time would become Southwick Road. From the west side of this little town was what became North Hylton Road. Almost every curve and change of direction of the river produced a little narrow tongue or spit of sand and debris, creating

Young people of today attending matches at the Stadium of Light will never realise the full significance of the large miner's lamp which stands adjacent to the ground. This photograph shows them what stood there before the Stadium was built – a great pit.

dangerous narrows which would require careful navigation even for a small river craft.

Flying on, our gull would observe an untouched river on both the north and south banks until reaching Hylton where settling on a rock he would observe the ferry which plied across the Wear. We will leave our seagull here as we carry on with our journey.

We are back at the time of the real foundation of Sunderland as it gradually changed from a fishing village to a centre for the export of coal, via the North Sea, as the exploitation of the Durham coal field began to gather momentum.

It was the necessity to bring coal down to the river mouth in the mid 1600s that would see the first concerted efforts to make the river easier to navigate and from then on the use of keelboats would begin. Road haulage was neither feasible nor economical to move large quantities of coal over totally inadequate roads from obscure inland colliery locations, so the keel was used to overcome this problem. One of my maternal great-great-great-grandfathers was Thomas Reed, listed as a keelman in the 1851 census. The river would be well cleared for shallow draught keels in his early career around 1810 or so. However, in the year 1600 it would be quite an obstacle course to negotiate, especially with a fully loaded keel and an ebbing tide with cross winds or dangerous river currents to contend with, plus a heavy load of coals. Each keel would carry approximately 18 tons of coal. They were built with wide flat bottoms and very shallow draught from keel to gunwale, plus large hatches for ease of loading and discharging their cargoes of coal. In the heyday of the keels our little river would be a very lively place indeed as there must have been great competition and camaraderie amongst these men. In 1786 the total coal shipments from the Wear equated to some 3,000 keelboat journeys up river and the same number down river, fully loaded.

However, today the keel, like the dinosaur is extinct, with coal very close behind them, yet for many years your ancestors and mine earned their living by plying their trade on our river of life. It now flows so peacefully that they and many more of our ancestors would not recognise it at all. Nevertheless in the year of 1600 the road to Sunderland was considered the road to nowhere, you came out where you went in and saw nothing worth while for your trouble. Yet by the 19th and 20th centuries the tables had been completely turned, for men of business came to Sunderland by the score, to sell chains, paint, steel pipes, copper pipes, steel plates, timber, anchors, paraffin, candles, oil and many other types of merchandise to the buyers from the shipyards, or engine works, forges, ships chandlers and shipping butchers.

All of this was a far cry from the small natural but awkward river of the 17th and 18th century when a traveller from would sail or row down a river filled with long forgotten place names. The Wear flows almost due north from Durham to Chester-le-Street then makes a great sweeping U-bend, in turning east on its journey to the sea. Then just before reaching South Biddick we come to an area called 'The Crossings'. We next arrive at 'Fosters Sand' opposite 'Worm Hill' with 'Worm Well' on the north bank. Then for 1,000 feet we traverse 'Cow Roads' which ends at 'Cow Road Nook' where the river bends into the 'Long Ratch', a straight stretch of river some 2,500 feet in length. As the river runs on we pass 'Nic Mushins Sand' with 'White-Hugh Stone' sitting in the bend of the river at Mr Lilburn's ground. We next arrive at 'Boild and Roast Ratch', quickly followed by another well known stretch of the river named the 'Sow and Piggs'. Just west of Hylton we find the 'Ferry Boat Sand' then just east of the ferry we locate the 'Brigg Stones'. Running on east we come to the 'Shoulds', quickly followed by 'Canch End' then 'Cyngdens Sand' with 'Megg's Hole' lying near the bank at 'Clacks Hugh'. 'Gaff le Sand' was a massive 2,000 foot bed of sand forming the south bank, west of 'Well Dock, Dean and Quay' on the north bank.

'Pallion Sand', complete with its spit, stood exactly where the north end of Alexandra Bridge would eventually be erected and opened in 1909. Then at the next curve downstream we find the usual spit of sand at 'Rabbit Hole Sand', which lay due south of Suddick, while the Deptford peninsular on the south side was dominated by the 'Reigh Sand'. 'The Ravens Wheele', 'Ravens Wheele Ratch' and 'Black Horse Sand' formed the river front for both Wearmouth Colliery and the present day Stadium of Light, while just round the curve was the Sheepfolds which still exists to this day. 'Tom Potts Rock' and the 'Stodden' were located just west of today's Wearmouth Bridge with the 'Pann Sand' sitting in mid-stream just opposite the present day University buildings. These are just some of the riverside place names which existed in the formative years of Sunderland and our river. Most of them have died out with the passing of time and changes in industrial usage by a changing population. The odd ones have survived the passage of time but they form a very small minority as the river was dredged and straightened for industry.

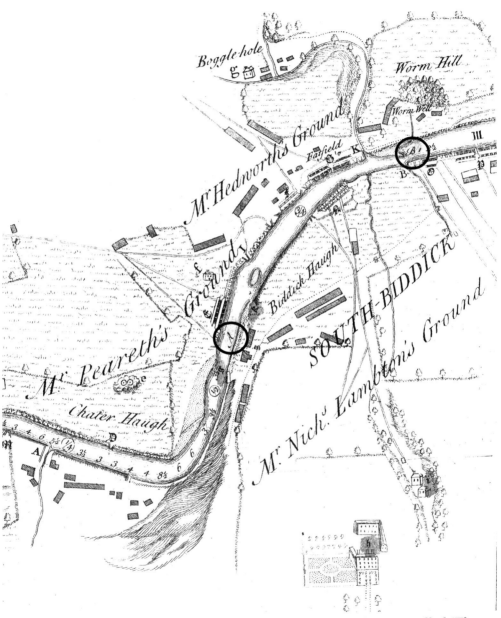

An extract from the Burleigh & Thompson map of 1737. The area called 'The Crossings' is circled in the centre; it is next to a staithe for loading keelboats. Below 'Worm Hill' and 'Worm Well' is 'Fosters Sand' (circled to the top right) which created a dangerous narrow on the river. At the bottom of the map is 'Biddick Hall' while just above, to the right, is 'Nich Lambton's Fire Engine'.

A lovely view of Deptford old quay and the new Queen Alexandra Bridge. The overhead gantries of Doxford's can be seen behind the south support column of the bridge. There is a wide variety of ships and cobles dotted about the river, including three wide, flat keelboats loading at the two staithes where the quay sweeps round. This shows keels were in use for a long time on the Wear.

Many small staithes existed in various parts of the river for handling small amounts of inland coal on its journey to the sea. This traffic would gradually build up with the passage of time as Sunderland grew into a major exporter of fuel to feed the world's first industrial revolution. This initial period of growth saw many families leaving the land for more lucrative work in the mines or as teemers and trimmers who loaded the coal ships from the newly built staithes. The teemers ran the coal into the shoots and then into the hold while the trimmers moved the coal to balance the ship in the water. The sons of these men would perhaps run away to sea as the taste for adventure bit into them as far horizons beckoned. Others would move into the riverside occupations associated with shipbuilding or the many ancillary trades that sprang from it as the development of the new port expanded. These formative years from 1600 onwards saw a period of rapid growth and expansion and housing became a prime necessity to accommodate the massive influx of people. Sunderland grew from its humble beginnings of a tiny row of fisherman's cottages into today's city of almost 300,000 people.

The vast financial involvement required to locate then gain access to the coal reserves lying under our feet was matched by the riverside entrepreneurs. Boat and keelbuilding, ropemaking, timber imports, glass production, brickmaking and a whole multitude of other trades and professions sprang up along the riverside. The population by and large would travel on foot, moving in a never ending and growing stream about our fledgling town and port. Horse-drawn traffic increased in direct proportion to the population, leading to the creation of many new businesses supplying food for both human and equine consumption. Fine weather made for easy travelling while rain created seas of mud in our streets and foot paths, if you were lucky enough to have one. The cart wheels and heavy feet of the horses churned up the roads, great deep ruts which soon filled up with rain water. Moving around Sunderland under those conditions requires some thought when we are used to having everything paved with either tarmac or concrete with street lights after dark and public transport, or private transport as the case may be. However, try and visualise the old streets three or four hundred years ago that our ancestors moved around in.

In the early 1700s there were several men of great skill and vision, such as Robert Shout one of the early engineers of the port. He worked to try and control our awkward river, building his piers in 1726, cleansing the river of shoals such as the Stell Canch and Sledway entrances through which all shipping had to enter or leave. He was followed by men such as John Murray who built our dock out into the North Sea, making it unique in British dock construction and one of the most brilliant pieces of marine civil engineering you could find. His system of immense 500 foot long half conical groynes, constructed in stone and mortar, set on and into the soft lime stone of the massive outcrop of the south rocks, trapped most of the tidal and sea borne sand and shingle moving along our coast, creating land when none had existed previously. Behind this man-created land he excavated our dock, using the excavated materials to supplement the sea borne sand and gravel. He then framed the whole dock in hard limestone, creating the quays and bridge entrances, sluices and gate housings. The west side of this new dock was designed to accommodate a great battery of coal staithes which could handle millions of tons of coal per annum. A great fleet of colliers or little coal carrying ships started sailing in and out as regular as clockwork, carrying the massive output of the Durham coal field to the far corners of the globe. The efforts of John Murray and his financial partner Sunderland's Member of Parliament, George Hudson, gave Sunderland 120 years of great sea trading in every commodity we could manufacture or win from the bowels of the earth.

The internal river, running westward from the harbour mouth, had seen an equal share in improvements and modifications but obviously on a much smaller scale. Many old quays sprang up like mushrooms to facilitate a whole variety of businesses and enterprises, including shipyards where many great builders have emerged over the last 300 years or so.

An old advert for Robert Thompson's shipbuilding enterprise shows his Southwick Yard top, and his Dock Yard at the bottom. The Dock Yard stood opposite where St Mary's car park is now – hard to visualise as the river and town is today.

THE BIRTH OF A TOWN

The *Sheaf Mount* is towed to the fitting out quay after its launch from
J.L. Thompson's.

Old Sunderland to me means the period of time from the years 1600 to 1750 which is the time our city was in its infancy. The twin forces of a rising coal exporting industry and forward thinking harbour and river custodians became the motivational factors in the rise of the area on the south bank of the River Wear. The earliest map I have shows our town as it was then from the Barrack Street area in the east, to Sans Street in the west, lining the river bank to the north, with Prospect Row and Coronation Street forming the southern boundary. The Town Moor at that time is almost L-shaped, running from the 35 foot high clay cliff at the river mouth, where the 1726 pier was built, then southwards to a break in the cliffs near the old Hendon Dock entrance. I notice that the area where St John's Church and School stood in my time is marked as Mr Meaburn Smith's house and gardens. Church Lane, which later became Church Street, and Sunderland Parish Church are both clearly marked. Near the church, on the site of the Assembly Garth, is listed the hospital and Town Hall. Running through what became Adelaide Place was a street marked as the Intake, which formed the southern boundary of the Town Moor.

My 1737 map of the River Wear, from its mouth almost to Chester-le-Street, is a mine of information. Drawn on linen by Messrs Burleigh & Thompson it is also a work of art. It shows four windmills on the north side of Coronation Street, between Church Lane and Sans Street, with the Pann Fields west of Sans Street. A coble landing is marked at the landward end of the pier, with the Custom House Quay to its west and the Low Ferry landing next to it. The high ferry landing is just above Bodlewell Lane while Low Street sits where it has always been, between High Street and the river. A small cluster of buildings stand at the junction of the south end of Sans Street and what became Borough Road. The area to the south is all open farm land, with no visible buildings of any kind or type.

To the west of the high ferry boat landing is the Road Stead, an obvious place for waiting or loading colliers to be berthed, with Wearmouth Burns just further west again. Travelling on inland we come next to the Salt Panns and the Pann Ferry, roughly lying where the old S.P. Austin's Shipyard and pontoon were located, and almost due north of the Sunniside Estate. A great sand bank sits in mid stream just east of the Road Stead, named the Pann Sand. Four sand banks sit at the mouth of the river, the largest being the Stell Canch with two channels. To the north side is the Stell with the Sledway on the south side, very near to the 1726 pier shown complete with its 14 foot thick protective sand bank. Just west of these sand banks, on the north shore, is the Ham Sand and the two beacons to guide ships in and out of the Stell. Between the east beacon and Roker Ravine, which isn't named, is a projecting point named Rocus Point, the possible forerunner of the name Roker as this area became known in later years.

The whole of the area on the north side of the river is only very lightly built up with great areas covered by hills of ballast. The name of Sir William Williamson is emblazoned across the whole tract,

This view of our bridges is taken looking down stream from Robert Thompson's Yard. It shows the railway bridge much as it is today but look at the road bridge behind it which has no cantilever suspension arch – it is the bridge dating from the 19th century.

including Monkwearmouth Town. There are three roads linking this town. One runs up from the river and the ferry which plied its trade across the Wear day after day for many many years. A second road runs to South Shields to the north. While the third runs north west via Suddick Town, now Southwick, linking in with the Hylton Ferry crossing road before travelling on to Newcastle. The remainder is all agricultural land with hedge rows clearly outlined and Monkwearmouth Church and Hall located midway between the river and little town. The north and south shores of our river are linked by a number of ferries at various points along the river bank up as far as Hylton.

My map of the river mouth for the year 1800 shows a very substantial fort built high on the top of the 35 foot high cliff, not very far from where the Welcome Tavern pub now stands. By 1850 my map for that time shows the fort gone and in its place stands a Barracks of considerable size. It was clearly remembered by all four of my grandparents and part of it very well known by myself. There is an old artillery gun battery sited at the river mouth to this very day. Gun ports were strategically placed and built in solid limestone with cast iron wheel runners set into the stone base for the guns to slew upon. The only thing missing are the guns themselves, which is a pity.

With the growth of the coal trade came a growth in population which in turn produced a need for more housing, plus the many other amenities which come as a natural progression for the people of the town. Then in 1796 a superb bridge, which was one of the wonders of the age, was opened linking the two sides of the river; with a road and foot means of access for both business and pleasure. It was the envy of the North East beating all other towns and cities to such a marvellous amenity. The bridge was built due to the generosity and foresight of one of Sunderland's greatest benefactors – Rowland Burdon – who contributed more than three-quarters of the cost from his own personal fortune. He is commemorated by having Burdon Road named in his honour, a small acknowledgement for such a great deed which put Sunderland at the forefront of the whole country with this magnificent bridge in 1796.

However, let me draw you back to our Sunderland of 1737 and try to recapture the essence of that time when primitive living conditions were the normal circumstances of our ancestors. The houses in many instances would be quite basic, often large tenements for the poorer classes, but more elaborate for the wealthy, just as it has always been. In 1737 Sunderland had no bridge, no exchange, no infirmary, no gas, no police and no waterworks, while in shipbuilding terms there were only three yards on the north bank and three on the south bank. The number of vessels belonging to the port in 1786 was 387, which increased to 981 by the year 1848, while the coal tonnage rose from 52,610 tons in 1786 to 198,937 tons in 1848. The ships built on the river at that time would carry about ten keels of coal. The keels negotiating the shallows while the colliers waited in the 'Road Stead' – between Wearmouth Bridge and today's Fish Quay – to be loaded. Roads and streets were unpaved and effluent was a major problem as sewers did not exist. Water was drawn from wells scattered around the area which were libel to contamination from ground seepage. This brought many types of diseases to people via their drinking water. Today we do not always appreciate the benefits of tapped water and flush toilets.

By the year 1777 High Street Bank had a high retaining wall, between Sans Street and George Street on the south side. The houses had a terrace in front of them extending a considerable way into the street. At the north side of this area was a wall with several steps leading down to the horse road which was on a much lower level. The raised terraces were called Batteries and several trees grew here which gave the place its name of High Justice Trees. The magistrates of the Burgh were in the habit of holding their meetings there. Eastward from George Street to Mauds Lane, on the south side of High Street, the ground was high, framing a sloping bank but not a terrace. At Mauds Lane, however, the terrace commenced again and ran along the foot of Gray Street. It extended some distance into the street and was on a much higher level than the other terrace. There was a descent of twenty steps into the road and this part of the street was called Low

One of the many little shipyards which sprang up along the banks of the Wear to build the little 100 tonners needed by the coal trade. When losses due to storms or running aground were quite common, it was the brave seamen who faced the harsh seas when they sailed out of our harbour with their cargos of coal.

Justice Trees. The principle thoroughfare from Bishopwearmouth to Sunderland was down Beggars Bank, then along Low Street which was the principle business centre of the town at that time. Beggars Bank later became Russell Street but received its original name from the fact that the Beadle of Sunderland Parish was stationed there to stop the ingress of vagrants who were likely to commit crimes in the town.

Previous to the opening up of ground at Bishopwearmouth for building sites, the most respectable inhabitants resided in the east end of the town with many fine homes in Low Street. As new streets were built they moved westwards and so the town grew. In 1777 the butchers' market was held in High Street between Queen Street and Church Street. The vegetable market was held further down the street. The first Act for paving, lighting and watching was obtained in 1809, but it wasn't until 1826 that a new market was commenced and this eventually became the old Market of my boyhood days. At the foot of Union Lane stood the Cross; around it and raised several steps above the street, were the Plain Stones where the butter and poultry markets were held. Also at the Cross was the pillory and stocks where convicted felons received a thorough pelting with rotten eggs and old fruit to degrade then publicly. In those days annual ass races took place in High Street and various other sports and amusements were held. The course was from Bishopwearmouth Church to Pann Lane. However, by 1782, regular horse races were held on the Moor, which was sufficiently extensive for the purpose, until building reduced its size and another site had to be found. There was bull baiting on Bishopwearmouth Green in early times which would attract large crowds until it was ploughed up by Thomas Liverseed using two mares to do the job in 1749.

The seaward end of High Street ended at the Coney Warren where Warren Street derived its name, but was part of the Moor then with the area called the North Moor. On this very ground was where the fishermen of the 18th century used to dry and repair their fishing nets much to the annoyance of the Freemen and Stallingers of the town. The dispute, based upon the fishermen's long free usage and ancient verbal rights, created an ongoing battle for many years. Apart from these fisher folk, the Moor was a moor in the truest sense without any development at all. The always intriguingly named Hat Case was built just west of the North Moor, but had vanished before my time, as had the once salubrious Fitters Row where the wealthy coal fitters once lived. They were the middle men of the coal trade. Their homes gave way to Rickaby Street flats and part of Harrison's Buildings. Nevertheless, I did run around the old area quite a bit as a boy and remember Silver Street quite well, with Bess Webb's shop and Swalwell's rag shop. My great-grandparents lived there during the 1881 census.

From the original small fishing village of around the year 1600 to the Parish of Sunderland with its new church of 1719, we can see continual growth as the town spread west, then north after the building of the 1796 bridge. Sans Street Mission was built two years earlier in 1793. The Elephant Tea House at the junction of Fawcett Street and High Street West was built in 1827, quickly followed by the old Eye Infirmary in 1836. Ulysses S. Grant, former President of the USA, was present at the ceremony for the laying of the foundation stone for our Museum in 1877. The Victoria Hall arose between the years 1870 and 1872. The Queen Alexandra Bridge was opened in 1909 to supplement the main Wearmouth Bridge which had been rebuilt in the 1850s, and again in the late 1920s, which is the bridge we use today. The bridge's legendary silver rivet installed by the Duke of York, who became George VI, was done with the help of two Sunderland men. The riveter was Jim Redpath and his hadder on was Jimmy Mitchinson, who were both East Enders.

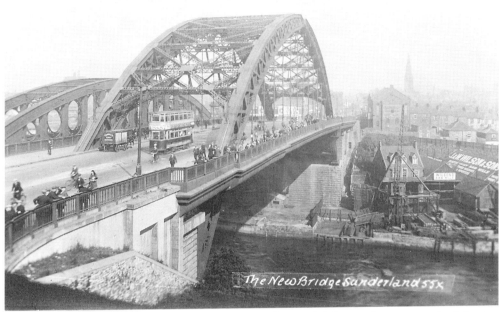

Two views of Wearmouth Bridge. *Above*: A few vehicles and many pedestrians – most dressed in flat caps and mufflers – cross the bridge in the late 1920s. *Below*: A modern view of the bridge and the pedestrians who use it. Sunderland supporters cross the bridge on their journey to the Stadium of Light.

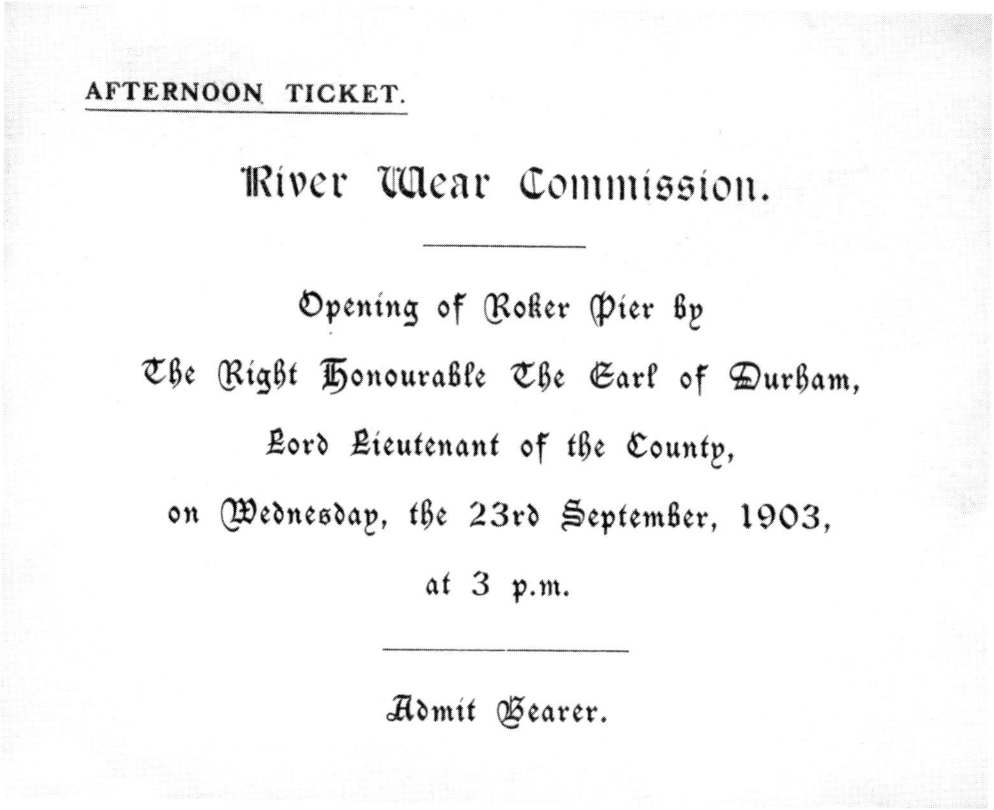

River Wear Commission.

Opening of Roker Pier by

The Right Honourable The Earl of Durham,

Lord Lieutenant of the County,

on Wednesday, the 23rd September, 1903,

at 3 p.m.

Admit Bearer.

These are copies of my grandfather's invitations to the opening of Roker Pier and celebration dinner given by Henry H. Wake to his staff and workmen who built his magnificent piers. He did not treat his staff like dogs as many do today and the results he obtained proved the value of his methods. The lowliest labourer got his dinner along with the chief engineer and they built him piers of outstanding use and beauty.

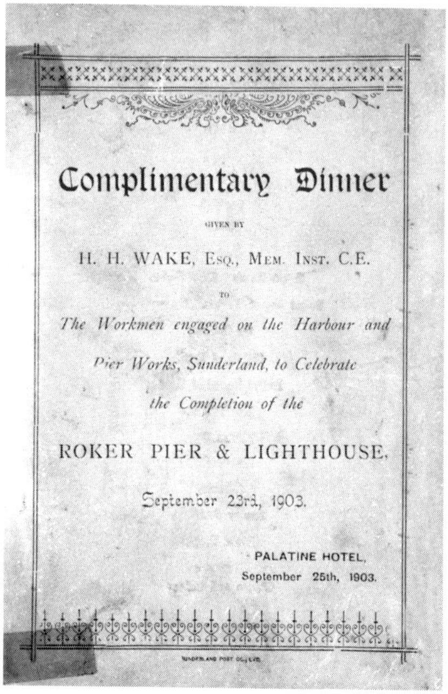

Complimentary Dinner

GIVEN BY

H. H. WAKE, Esq., Mem. Inst. C.E.

TO

The Workmen engaged on the Harbour and Pier Works, Sunderland, to Celebrate the Completion of the

ROKER PIER & LIGHTHOUSE,

September 23rd, 1903.

PALATINE HOTEL.
September 25th, 1903.

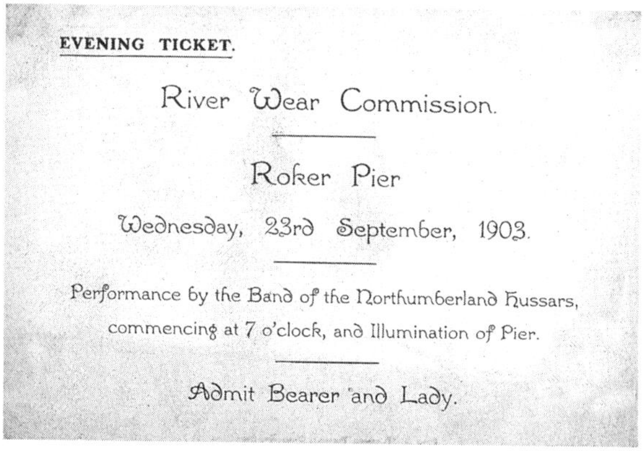

EVENING TICKET.

River Wear Commission.

Roker Pier

Wednesday, 23rd September, 1903.

Performance by the Band of the Northumberland Hussars, commencing at 7 o'clock, and Illumination of Pier.

Admit Bearer and Lady.

The expansion during my life time has followed the pattern of earlier years, westwards, ever westwards, with Humbledon, Grangetown, Plains Farm, Marley Potts, Springwell, Grindon, Thorney Close, Red House, Farringdon and Hylton Castle all rising in my time. Hylton with its ancient ferry links, which formed the main road to Newcastle from the early settlement of Bishopwearmouth, has been absorbed, likewise East Herrington, plus Silksworth, Ryhope, Fulwell, Seaburn, Houghton, right out to Hetton-le-Hole.

Yet for all of this massive growth there are two factors responsible for this immense development in less than 500 years – a vast coal field with a small heavily choked river in the middle of it. The driving force behind the river development was the sheer technical brilliance, courage, foresight and determination of the men involved. They are and were the real foundation stones upon which everything else depended. The other marine activity of shipbuilding was in truth only a secondary enterprise, yet it raised Sunderland to the very pinnacle of international fame and acclaim. I mention shipbuilding as secondary to coal and rightly so, however it was a tremendously powerful second. The industry grew from the little wooden sail driven 100 tonners to vast super tankers of enormous displacement, showing and proving the skills and great adaptability of both the management and work force on Wearside. The romance of sail was well and truly established on our river for I still marvel at the great achievements of ships such as the *Torrens*. To me she was the greatest wind driven ship ever built, proven on those dramatic long runs from England to Australia. She broke the then record with a trip of 64 days, repeated that feat several times and

A broadside launch from Robert Thompson's Bridge Dock Yard in the 19th century.

Robert Thompson's Southwick Yard.

holds it for ever as no other commercial sailing ship has ever beaten her times. She became a legend in her own lifetime with her brilliant ability to handle the rough seas of the Atlantic, Pacific or Southern Oceans, sailing through the most dangerous waters on the planet with consummate ease compared to other ships of her day. Although only one of many, she epitomises the shipbuilding skills of Wearside which helped to open up the world to the great benefit of our nation in our days of marine dominance.

Having missed the sailing shipbuilding era, I was able to witness quite a large slice of the steel era, as my maternal grandparents lived upon the docks. They resided at 'The Diver's House', South Docks, Sunderland, for almost 30 years. I was a constant visitor and still have my wartime docks' pass. Not many boys were lucky enough to have access to the docks during the war when 'Careless Talk Cost Lives'. So I kept my mouth shut as to what I saw happening. Bartram's Shipyard was just across the road from the Diver's House. J.L. Thompson's built at the North Sands Yard, just about where the Glass Centre is now, while S.P. Austin had their yard and pontoon just east of the bridge. John Crown had his yard at the Strand Slipway just west of J.L. Thompson's, right next to the Folly End. Laing's Yard was at Deptford and the *Torrens* was built there, as were many top class oil tankers in later years. Moving up stream we had the massive Doxford complex of six berths for shipbuilding, plus a superb engine works, just west of the Alexandra Bridge. Pickersgill's Yard was opposite on the north bank. The most westerly yard in my time was Short Brothers, above Doxford's on the south side of the river. This gave us eight top class shipyards and all with great reputations worldwide, which they guarded very jealously. When you add four more engine works to Doxford's, the list reads: North Eastern Marine Engine Works on the docks itself; George Clark's works at Southwick just east of the bridge; Dickinson's just up above the Manor Fitting Out Quay of J.L. Thompson's and below Wilson's Sawmills east of Wearmouth Bridge on the north bank; and finally the Scotia Engine Works just east of S.P. Austin's Yard on Low Street. These shipyards and engine works when taken in total added up to many thousands of jobs for the people of Sunderland, with a massive diversity of skills being created to carry out the technical side of shipbuilding and engineering. Forges and foundries existed at Copperas Bank Forge, Sunderland Forge and Engineering Company, Lynn's Foundry, Jenning's Foundry and Wear Winch. These were all dirty heavy industrial industries where cloth caps, mufflers, hobnail boots, fustian trousers or boilersuits were the order of the day when answering the 7-30 am buzzers which called the workers to labour every morning, come rain, snow or blow. The multitude of skills developed over the years was enormous and far too long to list. Some of them were: compass makers, radar mechanics, marine engineers, electrical trades, steel trades, wood trades and then there were the fourteen or fifteen-year-old boys heating rivets. Ladies grafted away in canteens to feed the work force and white collar draughtsman produced the detailed drawings required by all trades. Store keepers or buyers all contributed to the reputation of Sunderland as the greatest shipbuilding town in the world. I look back with great pride at your ancestors and mine who not only out-built the rest of the world but they also out-classed them for quality and service.

The covered yard at Doxford's in the final years of shipbuilding on the Wear.

Two views of the Queen Alexandra Bridge. The top picture shows part of Pickersgill's Yard on the north bank with Doxford's opposite and George Clark's Engine Works, top right. Below is a more up to date, and closer view, quite familiar to many today.

An illustration that formed part of an advert for Doxford's shipbuilding enterprise from the early 20th century.

Robert Thompson's Bridge Dock Yard at the end of the 19th century.

A Barclay diesel locomotive shunts wagons at Wearmouth Colliery in 1969.

The river has never slept during all of these formative years. The tide times governed all sailings, launches and transfers from the dock to the river and vice versa. The river pilots worked the tides, alongside the foyboatmen and tugboatmen so there was ongoing activity almost around the clock. Prior to the construction of the Corporation Quay there was virtually unlimited access to the south side of the lower river, as my 1896 map clearly shows with the main entrance to the docks running down North Moor Street, then along the water's edge behind the east perimeter of the Barracks, totally different to what became the entrance in my days. At the east end of North Moor Street were the Commissioners' Stairs. Built entirely of stone, they curved gently as they descended to the Commissioners' Quay which was the most easterly part of the old East End. There was a ferry landing right on the curve of the river and the south running cliff, with a slipway adjacent to the landing. Further west was the Pottery Bank, with the pottery building above and to the south west. The river front was made up of many small quays: Low Quay, Bowes Quay, Etterick Quay, Custom House Quay, Nobles Quay and Mark Quay all crammed in between the Commissioners' Stairs and the bottom of Church Street. In the early days, keels, skiffs and cobles, along with dozens of colliers, crowded the lower reaches of the river. Trades such as sailmakers were in great demand, along with ships chandlers and shipping butchers, who have

'Pyrex' at home

In this kitchen are so many things in 'Pyrex'! Mixing bowl, pie dishes, casseroles, rolling pin...in fact almost everything you need for preparing, cooking and serving hot foods, straight from the oven to table—and for chilling, storing and serving all your 'cold cookery' too! 'Pyrex' is practical and low-priced; smooth-finished and so easy to clean; cooks so much better—and quicker. 'Pyrex' brand is the name you know, the name you can depend on. So for your own protection, look for the name 'Pyrex' on every piece of oven-table glass

See the complete range of clear and coloured 'PYREX' in your shop

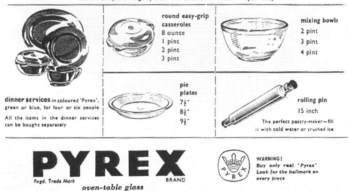

dinner services in coloured 'Pyrex', green or blue, for four or six people

All the items in the dinner services can be bought separately

round easy-grip casseroles
8 ounce
1 pint
2 pint
3 pint

pie plates
7½"
8½"
9½"

mixing bowls
2 pint
3 pint
4 pint

rolling pin
15 inch
The perfect pastry-maker—fill it with cold water or crushed ice

PYREX
Regd. Trade Mark
oven-table glass
BRAND

WARNING!
Buy only real 'Pyrex'
Look for the hallmark on every piece

MADE HERE IN SUNDERLAND BY JAMES A JOBLING & CO LTD · WEAR GLASS WORKS

As well as shipbuilding and coal mining, Sunderland was also famous for another industry – glass making. Here an advert from 1958 promotes the wares of James A. Jobling.

all but vanished in today's world. Unlike today these quays were strewn with chains, anchors, hawsers, hoists, sheer legs and all of the parafinalia necessary for the running of the port. Road haulage was almost totally horse-drawn or man-powered with a great variety of vehicles churning up the roadways with their narrow steel rimmed wheels, creating seas of mud in wet weather with both man and beast slipping and sliding as they tried to do their work. The only illumination in early times was either with candles or oil lamps and, failing that, then just the light from the fire in the living room if times were hard; which I suppose they often were for the poor of that time. Yet for all that, our folks struggled on and prospered in many cases by developing or adapting to new skills and techniques, especially in the shipbuilding industry. House building also progressed at a tremendous pace to keep up with the expanding population. There were also great improvements in sewers, piped water, gas supplies and electricity which added greatly to the quality of life. The advent of steam marked an amazing advance for our nation, yet that too, like our port and town, depended upon coal, the black gold won from the bowels of the earth by blood, sweat and tears. It created the world's very first railways right here in the North East of England, with men who were original thinkers leading the rest of our country forward into realms which were almost beyond belief. It is not beyond comprehension to say that modern science owes a lot to our northern skills and inventiveness, such as Robert Shout's first steam dredger used here on our river, a world first way back in our early history as both a port and a town.

A 1950 advert from the *Sunderland Echo* informing the public to use electricity outside peak-hours to help industry on Wearside.

FROM THE DURHAM COAL FIELD TO OUR DOCKS

Shotton Colliery.

A postcard view of one of the many coal mines in County Durham. Shotton Colliery was sunk in 1840 but was abandoned 36 years later. In 1900 it was re-opened and was worked for 72 years before it finally closed.

Once upon a time in the far western reaches of County Durham the native population discovered small outcrops of coal either at, or very near, to the surface of the ground. At the coast odd little seams were found, along with coal exposed and washed up on the beaches by the action of both tides and storms as they battered the coastline over long periods of time. It was discovered, probably by accident, that it was vastly superior to wood as a form of heating and was therefore extracted from the ground to be burned in homes for heating, cooking and boiling water. These early miners consisted of father, mother and children who created little drift mines as their labours took them further underground in search of this vital commodity. Their early experiences saw them developing new skills in the shoring and proping up of their little mine roofs, while the more skilful and better organised began to sink small shafts, creating what became known as bell pits. Being below ground level created water problems in wet weather, due to seepage and draining. Young children were often forced into employment, many working in abominable and dangerous conditions with the most basic tools and lighting it is possible to imagine. The winters were long, dark and very cold. Homes were primitive in the extreme and coal made the difference between life and death in our cold northern climate when comfort was almost unknown. These early miners laboured long and hard, often wearing themselves out in the process. Life expectancy was often quite short due to the complete lack of any medical knowledge or facilities to succour them in times of illness and sickness.

We today cannot conceive how harsh life was for these early miners. They lacked every amenity we take for granted today, living on a spartan diet in their wattle and daub shelters or caves if they could find them local to their pits or drift mines. They were dirty and covered in coal dust, completely illiterate as schools did not exist for them, yet they nevertheless founded an industry which would become a giant. That giant created our City of Sunderland, producing the drive and initiative for our forefathers to develop the port expressly for the purpose of shipping coal. The knock-on effect of coal saw the development of the world's first steam engines from which in time grew the railways for the transporting of the 'Black Gold' in massive quantities from the pit head to the teeming shoots on the docks. Then it was transported to any part of the world via the little 100 or 500 ton sailing vessels built on the Wear for that specific purpose.

I have a map of the Durham coal field which is staggering in its scope and complexity. Undated, it lists approximately 25 separate coal companies, covering roughly 200 different collieries sited within a 28 mile radius of our port. These mines were all linked by rail, a fantastic feat of surveying and civil engineering, focusing the vast output of the Durham coal field upon our port. As the industry grew so did new techniques and safety procedures, due to the inherent danger in the industry which existed from day one right through to the closures of the 1980s and '90s. It bred a special type of man with a language of his

This famous illustration by Thomas Hair, first published in 1844, shows the coal staithes at Galley's Gill. The original 1796 bridge can be seen in the background. After the staithes were opened the keelmen rioted here as they feared the drops would make them redundant. The Dragoons were called from Newcastle to quell the riot.

own special world which only a few outsiders were privileged to understand.

Step into the cage at the pit head surrounded by steel girders, muck, and grime. Hear the gates slam shut with you and your marras packed like sardines. Feel the chains tighten on the top of the cage in tension, then down you go 1,250 to 1,300 feet into the bowels of the earth. Once down at the shaft bottom you climb into a man-rider which runs you out maybe three miles under the North Sea. Then you leave that and jump on to a moving conveyor belt, to run out another two and a half miles. Jump off that and walk or crawl the final distance out to the coal face. All this before you had struck a bat of work at seven miles from the shaft bottom. Our coal field was several layers of long buried primaeval forest, eventually petrifying into coal. It was said that as we sat in front of our fires on cold winter evenings that we were feeling the heat of the primaeval sun, a brilliant analogy of something we took for granted. The development of our vast coal field, allied to steam propulsion, created our modern world and the technology we all take for granted. However, it was obtained at a price by men working in horrendous conditions.

The Durham coal lies in an almost crescent shape beneath both land and sea. The seams are thin as they run away both north and south into both Northumberland and Yorkshire with the greatest and thickest seams lying in our old county of Durham. Most collieries hit several seams in their search for the best and easiest coal to extract, often going down to 1,400 feet or so hitting seams such as the Five Quarter Seam, or the often quoted Hutton Seam.

One of the greatest problems for deep shaft pits was the need for air as neither man nor horse could survive let alone work without it. Many methods were tried over the years. From primitive beginnings in little drift mines or bell pits there arose a massive highly mechanised industry employing thousands upon thousands of men and boys. The hewer hewed the coal and the putter loaded the tubs. This was the start of a journey from the mine workings, over iron rails to the bottom of the shaft, to be raised and reloaded to continue its journey. It was pulled along by some grimy old locomotive and then into the main rail system. Eventually our coal would arrive at some staithe on Sunderland Docks, run down a gradient on to the actual drops, have the bottom holding pins knocked out of the truck for the coal to slide down the shoot and into the hold of some collier. The lights of London too were illuminated by the heat of the primaeval sun as our coal fed the heat into the boilers at Battersea Power Station which in turn raised the steam to drive the North East invented steam turbines which in turn drove the generators to produce London's electricity. The year 1904 saw nearly five million tons of coal leave the River Wear and most other years followed a similar pattern. The year 1927 saw five and a

Here we have a picture of coal being loaded into the hold of a collier which is lying at number 23 coal staithe in the south west corner of the Hudson Dock.

half million tons leave our port, proving our worth and making Sunderland a town of considerable national importance.

As we travel around the area today almost every village we pass through would have had a coal mine in the 19th century. Some were drift mines driven into hillsides while others were deep shafted mines. The traditional winding gear towered above the colliery with their massive wheels turning as the cages were raised or lowered, carrying either men or coal as the case may be.

Not for us the idyllic rustic rural farming village with ducks floating on ponds and chickens scratching around at the road side while roses grew around every door. Our villages were based upon power and technology, being dark and satanic, creating a race of men who raised Britain to the peak of industrial supremacy by extracting coal from the bowels of the earth. The miners at the sharp end were backed up by engineers, who's training and energy produced a steady flow of massive mechanical developments, improving the efficiency of everything related to the mines. One such man was Sir Humphry Davy who was commissioned to design a safety lamp that could be used in the mines without igniting the fire damp gases that had caused so many deaths in underground explosions. His Davy safety lamp was a great success, enabling miners to work in greater safety. The Davy lamp did not get rid of the gases, only one thing could do that – ventilation. Ventilation had been an ongoing problem throughout the

In almost every Durham mining village was the local 'store'. This postcard view shows the Medomsley Branch of the Annfield Plain Co-operative Society. Miners and their families bought everything they would need from the Co-op which boasted it catered 'from the cradle to the grave.'

entire history of mining, but like all things it too was eventually solved by the electric fan, and an up cast and down cast twin shaft in many mines.

The invention of coke by Abraham Darby in 1740 allowed cheap iron to be produced for the first time. Everything from then on hinged upon coal to make coke and coke to make steel, which provided rails, locomotives and all of the inventions which arose from this very strong and versatile material. The mines worked virtually 24 hours every day and needed constant care and maintenance to function safely and efficiently. It was always a high risk business with danger just around the corner for the unwary or careless man. The pullers and drawers who were responsible for all the shoring work in the mine had a saying: 'Pullers and drawers do not get hurt, they get killed' – a harsh but true safety philosophy with which to impress upon other men working with them.

The true mining village is no more but the legacy of those harsh working days still lingers in some forms of their village life. Their cricket teams still play regularly in our local leagues, as do their many football teams. Their leeks are world famous and a wonder of horticultural skill, with vegetable and flower shows adding a rich flavour. They enjoy their whippets and greyhounds and some of the greatest pigeon fanciers the world has ever seen live or have lived in North East pit villages. Races with over 30,000 pigeons competing attracts visitors from as far afield as Japan to obtain their bloodlines.

Music was a very popular past time in the Durham pit villages and many collieries had their own bands. Here is the South Moor Colliery Silver Prize Band who were winners of the Grand Shield at the Crystal Palace contest of 1907.

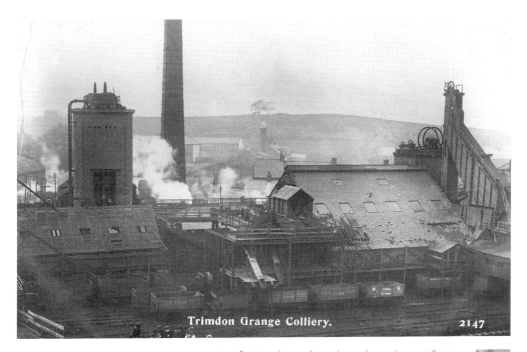

Trimdon Grange Colliery. 2147

The Durham coal field witnessed many tragedies. One disaster occurred at Trimdon Grange Colliery on 16th October 1882 when 74 men and boys were killed following an explosion. The pitman's poet, Tommy Armstrong, wrote a song to raise funds for the families of the miners who lost their lives. The song, *The Trimdon Grange Explosion*, is still sung today – such is the power of the words and the message behind them.

Right: The Trimdon Grange Colliery Banner.

The next time you pass the ski slope going up Silksworth Lane, try and remember this image of what was there before the slope was created. This was a typical deep mine shaft, right on our doorstep, where men toiled in the depths for many years.

The miners came out of the hole in the ground as black as the coal they raised, bathed in front of the living room fire in a tin bath, supported their wives and families, and washed the grime out of their throats with a pint or two of good strong ale.

The coal came here to Sunderland for shipment and our superb docks and port were created for that one purpose. My visions of this whole area started when I was wheeled down in my pram to my grandparent's house right next to the Sea Lock entrance from the dock. It is awash with memories, however memories only last a lifetime. I never heard many people mention John Murray in any great detail whatsoever. His design was revolutionary to say the least, winning a massive dock from the North Sea, and the worst the elements could throw against him. I can only stand with mouth agape, full of awe and wonder, at this long forgotten man of genius, who's skills and ability opened up the Durham coal field to its fullest potential, a monumental achievement by any standard.

His dock became known as the Hudson Dock due to the financial and entrepreneurial skills of our MP, George Hudson, in promoting the daring plans of John Murray. It was George Hudson who drew up the prospectus of the proposed Sunderland Dock Company which was published in 1845. The shares were quickly taken up and the requisite notices given to Parliament. A Bill was introduced in the next session which passed through the House of Commons on 2nd April and the

Lords on the 7th May. It received Royal Assent on 14th May 1846. This Act empowered the Sunderland Dock Company to execute all of the works connected therewith. The number of shares issued was 12,000, and the estimated expense of the project was forecast at £300,000, a massive sum in those days. The company was authorised to borrow an additional £100,000 if needed. Those amounts would run into many many millions of pounds today yet George Hudson never hesitated, working tirelessly for his constituents. His flair and persuasive manner soon saw the complete issue of shares taken up. Some of his many speeches show his absolute grasp of the situation and the multitude of benefits this new dock would bring, not only to the port and town's people, but also the whole coal field and surrounding area. His commitment was absolutely total and I doubt any port in the world had two greater champions working for it than John Murray and George Hudson.

These two men dominate 19th century Sunderland for me. Their combined aim was not to just build a dock, they wanted to build a dock which would make Sunderland into one of the foremost ports in the British Empire. The enormous fact to emerge with hindsight is that they succeeded in all of their plans as millions of tons of coal went down the shoots of the new coal staithes and continued doing so for over 100 years, making their venture truly monumental indeed. John Murray not only designed this entire project he also calculated the total costs involved and he carried out the whole enterprise within his financial estimates of the scheme, which in itself is another magnificent feat. He was a fantastic engineer by any standard.

Everything protruding from the main land mass in this picture is man-made ground, won from and against the sea by men of brilliance and determination – John Murray, the superb civil engineer and George Hudson, the town's then MP, who raised the money to finance the whole project. Their work allowed our dock and river to export over five million tons of coal per annum regularly in the 20th century. Their skill and actions actually made Sunderland, for without this dock the coal trade would have gone to the Tyne and Tees.

It is now some 64 years since the outbreak of the Second World War but these years stand out in my mind as the Hudson Docks became a real hive of activity. The war effort grew in momentum and the shipping increased to keep pace with the demands of industry and commerce. One of my many tasks at this time was to take my grandparents' grocery delivery from the Co-op store in High Street East, where Mr Keithley was the manager, down to my granny's house on the dock, a task I really looked forward to. Every tide saw an influx of ships into the port and the departure of many more to sea. There was coal, oil, petroleum, wood, etc, coming and going. Convoys formed off the mouth of the river for safety as U-Boat attacks could, and did, happen at any time of the night or day. Then, later in the war, truck load after truck load of munitions began to arrive at the East Quay just outside of our house. Then the loading of the convoys for Russia began with the five cranes working virtually 24 hours a day, loading tanks, bombs, shells, aircraft and a host of other items into our home-built Empire Boats to make what was without doubt the most hazardous sea journey of the entire Second World War. Those winter convoys must have been sheer hell with biting cold winds sweeping down from the North Pole and sea temperatures so low that a man was dead in two minutes if he was thrown overboard or blown into the sea by a shell or torpedo.

The black out was imposed to frustrate enemy aircraft and to save our lives in their bombing attacks. It made the docks a very dangerous place, especially for people who were strangers, but we knew it like the back of our hands. So we helped many strangers during these difficult years when we were fighting for our lives. Every sound became very accentuated in the total blackness. The ships were moved by the tugs with virtually no lights showing. The sound of a screw tug became very recognisable from a paddle tug as they manoeuvred a collier through the dock gates then into the middle basin, or half tide basin to give it its correct title.

There is a real and tangible reminder of these times in our own cemetery at Grangetown where in amongst the war graves are two which commemorate the deaths of Canadian sailors, one from HMCS *Arrowhead* and the other from HMCS *Eyebright*. Both of these young men were drowned in the dock after losing their way in the blackout. It never happened again as my grandparents took it upon themselves to meet the last bus from the town each night, then escort the entire shore party safely back to their two frigates which were built by John Crown of the Strand Slipway for the Canadian Navy. These two ships were fitting out at the Boilershop Quay of the North Eastern Marine Engine Works. Their crews went on 'Sippers' which meant they did not take their full rum ration. What they saved came to grandfather each week, while grandmother received a box of very valuable groceries, which were marvellous to us after being on our ration diet. Every so often I pop in and pay my respects to these two Canadians when I visit my own family graves. They came to fight with us and gave their lives for the cause. I remember them although I never actually knew them. They lie only a few hundred yards from their shipmates' guardians, my old grandparents.

For most of the war, every evening just as dusk approached, a lone Lockheed Hudson aircraft would fly up the coast about two hundred yards out from the beach and only two or three hundred feet above the sea. If I was on the dock, and heard him coming, then off I would run to the seaward end of the Sea Lock. Up he would come out of the south, while a proud 12-year-old stood waiting and waving, wishing he too could go with them spying on German shipping movements off the Norwegian coast.

There were several anti-aircraft batteries strategically placed around the docks. Also all of the merchant ships had some sort of armament, ready to hit back both at night or in daylight if the Luftwaffe paid us a visit. This was my dock as a boy and I was fortunate to behold many fascinating things as I absorbed every facet of men working. There was

Pit props from Scandinavia arrived by the shipload as regular as clockwork. They were then transported to the many mines around the old county of Durham. These dockers are bundling them up before the slings are wrapped around them. Then the crane was hooked on and the props were swung ashore into waiting trucks or stacked in great towers 20 to 25 feet high, ready and waiting for when they were needed.

the turner at his lathe, watching the revolving steel turnings coming spiralling from the cutting tool, as he checked with his callipers that all was well. Then there were squads of dockers, or stevedores to give them their correct title, swinging their hooks to grasp and impale bales of sisal, or humping props around. There were platers mounting the plates on to the frames of the ship, ready for the riveters to follow on, and shipwrights trimming pine deck deals with a adze, a very skilled job. There were the crane drivers climbing up to their cabins on high, luffing and slewing their jibs with brilliant accuracy. Then there was my old grandfather who carried on because of the war until his 71st year, diving at any hour of the night or day to keep the war effort going. This was my dock, alive and vibrant just as its two great creators, Murray and Hudson, envisaged and as I so affectionately remember it, even after all of these many and changing years.

My mother's family looked upon it as their spiritual home as I still do. 'I'm going down home,' meant only one thing, they were going to a house on John Murray's land, won from the cold harsh North Sea. His skills were written across its broad acres, with underground culverts along and under the East Quay, which carried the electrical power for the cranes, plus water and gas supplies. There was the massive turn tables and enormous hydraulic controls for his bridges, which opened and closed with the smoothness of silk. There were also great round fat bollards for mooring ships, with little tank engines chugging around, which was all taken for granted by every one who used the docks. But I also remember the many hidden things which many did not and have not seen. These are my memories and visions of this brilliant civil engineer Murray, who lies in Sutton Cemetery in Surrey but who's memory should be enshrined and emblazoned with prominence somewhere within our city of today. Of our MP, George Hudson, what

I love this picture of the old sea lock, simply because it shows my ancestral home. The Diver's House on the left of the picture was my ancestral pile, and I would not have changed it for the grandest

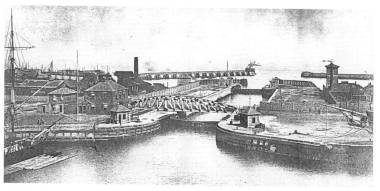

palace in the land. Grandfather and grandmother lived there until 1946. I had the most enjoyable childhood, escaping into the unknown recesses of the magical place so full of interest which has stayed with me all of my adult life. His diving suit is in Sunderland Museum and has been seen by many of his eleven children's descendents.

can we say, but thank goodness for a man of such vision and energy, who's financial skills underpinned a brilliant engineer.

These are my views of our docks which created so much work and therefore so much wealth for both the people of Sunderland and the Durham coal field. It is only with the benefits of age and maturity that one begins to realise how the actions of someone remote from your small world can affect your life, without you ever realising it. Yet the miner at Hetton or Eppleton Colliery became dependant upon John Murray's Docks to ship his coal, hewn from the depths of the Durham coal field, to the markets of the world. While in reverse the Sunderland Docks relied upon Hetton and Eppleton coal to keep its railmen, teemers, trimmers, tugboat men and merchant seamen in jobs at one and the same time.

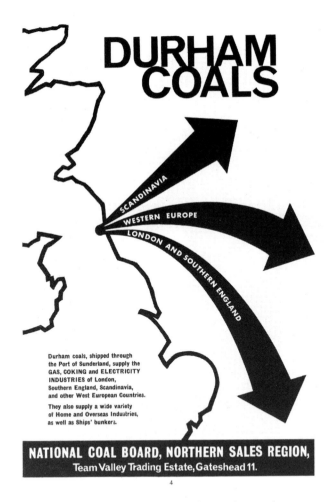

A National Coal Board advert from the early 1960s showing the importance of Sunderland in exporting coal throughout Europe.

Quite a lot of the main stonework is still intact within the fabric of our docks. The old Dock Head Office, though in a sad state, is still worth saving. The Gladstone Bridge is badly in need of chipping and scraping, then given a couple of good coats of paint, which should be done as soon as possible. However, the remainder has been rather badly neglected by the people appointed as our trustees. Yet the vast amount of work this dock created has never been weighed in its favour when it comes to financial considerations for its maintenance. We should remember its years of brilliant service to our ancestors, town and now city.

This old postcard shows John Murray's Dock Head Office and the Gladstone Bridge. The bridge was built around 1850 and is still standing proud but badly neglected and very sad looking. Our magnificent docks were built in just two short years using a technique which astounds me in its brilliance and uniqueness. Acres of land were won from the sea to create the most enormous amount of wealth for thousands of Sunderland folk and many other thousands from the county's massive mining community.

WARTIME MEMORIES

Cadet pilot James D. Taylor in training to become a Second World War fighter pilot. He first flew Beaufighters and then Mosquitos with the Strike Wing of Coastal Command where he won the DFC for Valour and rose to the rank of Flight Lieutenant.

Glimpses of the First World War

The National Kitchen at the bottom of High Street East provided good, well cooked food for both child and adult, way back when this photograph was taken around 1918. My mother is standing on the left with Susie Anderson, third from the right. Other names I remember from my mother's conversation are: Rosie Pratt and Lizzie Brown, but which ones they are I am not sure.

A photograph may be only a photograph to many people, but this one meant a lot to Margaret Oxley of Wear Street. It was sent to her four brothers in France during the First World War, when a letter could take a week or a month to reach home. One brother never came back, another died as a result of the war, while two survived, but they all carried a photograph of their youngest sister in their tunic pockets – this picture.

Luke Thompson somewhere in France during the First World War with his pair of horses which helped to draw a field gun. He survived the entire war and later worked with the boilermakers at the North Eastern Marine Engine Works, then lived to reach the grand old age of 94.

A group of local sailors who served on HMS *Broke*. Leading stoker George W. Thompson – from Sunderland, sitting left – was lost at the age of twenty-one, when his ship was torpedoed at sea during the First World War.

The seasons of the year were marked with various phases: tops and whips would have a run, hitchy quoit for girls, skates next, diablos, crackers, deligo, kick the tin and skipping ropes which would bring our mothers out and communal skipping would be the order of the day, with everyone joining in. Even our mothers would recapture their youth and in they would go with their pinafores held in their hand, with whoops and laughter. They were great times, great people, lovely days. But all of this was to come to an abrupt end on the 3rd September 1939, when we heard the air raid sirens for the first time which put the whole country on a war footing; heralding many great changes to all of our lives. The first effect for my brother and me was when we were evacuated along with thousands of other school children. We entered upon the longest journey of our lives up to that time which carried us from a massive town full of heavy industry to a remote village deep in the peaceful Yorkshire countryside, where the loudest noise you heard was the clip clop of the horse hooves on the road. It was a bit of a culture shock at the time, but we ended up in a nice lodge. We went to

This man in his diving gear, which is on display in Sunderland Museum, is my maternal grandfather Ralph Scott. He worked on many major underwater projects from the turn of the 20th century until he retired in 1946, when in his 71st year. He lived upon the South Docks for almost thirty years. I was taken down in my pram then lifted out and put into the punt to watch him descend into the murky depths, amidst a great shower of bubbles. When the war broke out in 1939, he decided that he wouldn't retire that December when he was 65 but would carry on and do his bit for King and Country, which he did in brilliant style without any fuss or bother. To go diving until that age strikes me now as a very brave thing to do, showing his love of country, family and friends in our hour of darkest need. In his youth and early manhood he had been a great

local footballer, playing with Raich Carter's father amongst others while winning the Wearside League four consecutive seasons, the magnificent Shipowners Cup three times – including the first year of competition – and the Monkwearmouth Charity Cup three times. A great fan of Winston Churchill, he too supported the war effort in his old age, just like his much admired Prime Minister. He never missed a call to dive, come hail, snow or blow.

the village school, saw conkers for the very first time in our lives and scrumped apples. We told our host, who was quite elderly, what the sea was like as he had never been near it in his entire life. We tried to settle down in the peace and quiet. Things went well until our father came to see how we were after about six months. He seemed quite happy about our circumstances until he asked my young brother a question. He turned to me and said, 'Who is he?' Father nearly had a stroke. His five year old son had forgotten him in six months. The result of this situation was to see us brought home. With no air raids taking place we were becoming complacent, but it was the lull before the storm which was to make Sunderland the seventh most heavily bombed town in the country.

I had in all truth had a foretaste of the Germans before the war actually started. It came about through my grandparents living on the Docks. My grandfather used to walk off most nights for a few pints in the King's Head pub which stood at the top of the Dock Bank. Quite often he met and had the company of the German captain of the *Cora* on these evening strolls. This man sailed his weekly boat from Bremerhaven to Sunderland regularly for many years and with the war imminent knew when his last visit was to be made. He invited our family on board for tea on a Sunday afternoon as a gesture of goodwill

Winston Churchill was only afraid of losing one battle and that was the Battle of the Atlantic which would have starved us into submission. To this end he sent his wife to Sunderland to encourage our shipbuilders to even greater efforts. We responded by sending ship after ship down the slipways into the Wear. From there they went out on the life-saving journeys for our nation.

and also to thank grandfather for his friendship over these years, giving me, a nine year old boy, memories which would last a lifetime. His parting gifts to me were a handful of German Gold Dollar Cigarette Cards which I still have. They show the build up of the Third Reich, which I did not fully understand at the time. I also didn't understand the significance of the large framed photograph of Adolf Hitler which adorned the main saloon wall. The German captain sailed away and out of our lives until about the middle of the war, when Lord Haw Haw in one of his many propaganda programmes gave out the full details of the show currently on view at the Empire, including the details of the cast etc. My grandfather swore until his dying day that only one German in the entire world was capably of providing that information. The captain, who knew our river entrance and port layout like the back of his hand. We spent many an hour wondering if he had come ashore from a U-Boat then spent the evening at the Empire just to shock us and prove how clever and skilful the Germans were at infiltrating our defences. That is a true story which became part of my family folklore for many years.

Access to the docks was restricted during the war and only holders of official River Wear Commissioners' passes could enter this restricted area. I still have mine, a circular brass disc, numbered 4906, which gave me access every week to carry my grandparents' groceries down for them.

The docks drew me like a magnet and I was always going down to visit and play. My grandfather lived adjacent to the Sea Lock in the

A relic and permanent reminder of events from 1939 – my dock pass.

house next to the Dock Master who was Captain Chapman who lived with his wife and two daughters. The dock police were in their office on the opposite side of the Sea Lock and the *Fire King,* a floating fire engine, was moored just below.

During the bombing of Sunderland the number 19 coal staithe was hit and put out of action. Then they just missed the Sea Lock bridge, blowing our motor boat to smithereens when the bomb struck the steps and quayside. Their next strike was the gates of Greenwell's repair dock that set the bunkering oil storage tank alight, spilling the burning fuel on to the water near the river mouth. There were two direct hits on the North Eastern Marine Engine works which were the largest engine works in the world when they were opened in 1868. These were the only hits on dock installations that I can remember which proves how inaccurate the German bombs were, especially at night when they damaged many domestic premises, but not many industrial ones. I remember seeing cargo ships brought to Greenwell's dry docks to be converted into miniature aircraft carriers to protect the Atlantic convoys. Others had been struck by torpedoes and had blow holes through then big enough to allow a double decker bus to drive through them.

Then of course I must mention the massive output of our shipyards during the war. It was phenomenal to say the least with Empire Boats

These four old school pals from Moor Board School all met up at the height of the Second World War and this lovely photograph commemorates the meeting. The sailor at the back left is Billy Wickham who joined up in 1938 and served the entire war in most theatres, and all classes of warships, ranging from Tommy Sopwith's yacht to ending up as the captain's coxswain on the battleship *Queen Elizabeth*. Next to him is Jimmy Taylor. Front left is Pop Stubbs and all I know about him is that his mother kept a pie shop in Burleigh Street. Front right is Billy Scott who served in the Fleet Air Arm on aircraft carriers in the North Atlantic, and he was my mother's youngest brother. Only Billy Wickham is still alive to tell the tale of those stirring times, and I thank him for his help.

leaving the slipways at regular intervals to try and keep up with the heavy losses we sustained due to the Atlantic U-Boat attacks. Now, looking back, I realise what a mighty effort we on Wearside put into the war. It was nothing to see men working three half shifts plus Saturday and Sunday. That was just overtime on top of their normal 48 hour working week. A half shift was from 5.30 pm to 9.00 pm, with 7.30 am until 4.00 pm on both the Saturday and Sunday, which equates to a total working week of $73^{1}/_{2}$ hours. The women folk also answered the call, making a very significant contribution in shipyards, factories, offices, roperies or on the buses and trams, and many other places. Everyone took the bombing and loss of sleep in their stride without any whining or complaining. It was a brilliant and very well sustained effort over six years in duration by the old men and women we see sitting in old folks homes today, and maybe even your grandmother or grandfather, but that is the way it was.

Living at the top of the Dock Bank during the bombing was not the safest of places. We had two direct hits in Barrack Street which killed quite a few people, including the whole Thompson family of two adults and two children. Next door, Ruth and Joan Crawford were buried alive for a long time before they were rescued from the debris of their home. Mr and Mrs Howard, the licensees of the Scotch Thistle pub, were also killed but their son survived, while the whole street was covered up to a foot deep with soil, wood, bricks, tiles and many other broken objects. Yet through it all the will never faltered. The people took it on the chin then braced themselves for the next round. My father lost his beloved canaries and our dog started to take fits due to a blast which was about 100 yards way. Then the next time it rained we were flooded out because the roof was full of holes, but what did that matter, we were alive and well. We were the lucky ones so what was a minor flood in the house to worry about.

These circumstances never ever leave you completely. In the early morning of 24th May 1943 Billy Miller came as close to death as it is possible to be without actually dying. He was in the Lodge Terrace air raid shelter which received a direct hit from a quarter ton high explosive bomb and lived to tell the tale. This shelter served the little community of Lodge Terrace at Hendon, many of whom were the families of railway men. Seventeen of them were killed and 36 were seriously injured, with ages ranging from 6 to 67 years. Due to the censorship regulations in force during the war, the names of everyone involved were never published but Mr Miller has rectified that omission in his marvellous first-hand account of the whole tragic circumstances. Yet for all the trauma, Mrs Mary Sweeting, who was trapped for many hours under tons of concrete and rubble, survived and lived until she was just four months short of her 100th birthday. My wife lost her playmate in Kathleen Harris and her sister Alice, who were both killed in that shelter. It was a dreadful blow to many families but the true heroism of the people stands out as a fitting memorial to everyone involved who paid the full price of war in this incident.

This photograph is of my cousin and namesake, Jackie Curtis, who was nineteen years of age when the Second World War broke out. He had served in the Merchant Navy since virtually leaving Moor Board School at fourteen. Our Jack was a real hero to me because he never missed a ship, even though he had several sunk under his feet. He came and stayed with us between ships. He knocked us out of bed at 3 am one morning, coming all the way from Malta only wearing a pair of shoes, trousers and an old coat. We took him in and sat round the kitchen table drinking tea before we put him to bed. He crossed the Atlantic a few times, then in April 1943 he sailed for Liverpool to join Convoy ONS5 to cross once more to bring the vital food and supplies we needed to survive and fight the war. This convoy was made up of 42 merchant ships which ran into a storm when several days out and was eventually detected by the German U-Boats around 28th April. The signal went out and a Wolf Pack of 34

U-Boats gathered to await the convoy in the mid-Atlantic, south east of Greenland, where they strung out in a great arc with others coming to join them. Over an eight day period, allowing for the dreadful storm, these U-Boats sank thirteen of our ships, including the SS *North Britain* with our Jack on board. I have mourned him these past sixty years. His was a quiet unseen and unheard bravery, earned in the most hideous battleground in the entire Second World War. The Battle of the Atlantic was fought against an unseen enemy in the dark, cold waters of a violent ocean. That is the story behind this photograph of an average looking man who earned my admiration and love which lasts to this very day.

I remember going to see my father at the Warden's Post one lunchtime. The sirens sounded for a daylight raid, in fact the day they hit Laing's Shipyard. We went up on to the roof to see what was happening and saw the Hurricane flight from Usworth shoot down the German bomber which plunged into the sea just north of the north pier where the wreck was. A few minutes elapsed before we saw the dingy with the crew in it. Then the Pilot Cutter went out and captured them, eventually bringing them off the dock where a large crowd had gathered to see a lorry come out through the gates. The Germans were sat with their backs to the cab while our soldiers with fixed bayonets stood guard over them. There was cheering for our triumph and booing for the airmen, with some old women, who may have lost sons in the First World War, spitting at them and shaking their fists. But generally it was quite good humoured as we have always been magnanimous in victory.

Our town, as it was then, became the seventh most heavily bombed in the war. Most important centres of shipping or aircraft production took a hammering from the Luftwaffe as Germany tried to kill us off by starving our forces of the tools and new equipment they needed. They

This little trader, the *Tyneholme*, knew its way in and out of Sunderland blind folded. She had the most distinct siren and should she blow it today I would know it was her. But she won't for she, like many others, was sunk by enemy action in the Second World War. She is seen here lying at the old number 21 coal staithe, obviously taking coal into her stern hold by the way she is lying. It is a permanent reminder of my boyhood every time I look at this photograph.

used flares to illuminate their targets, or incendiary bombs to create fires, plus of course the dramatic 1,000 pound bombs with their high explosive contents which made a mess of everything, bursting water mains, damaging underground cables, gas mains, telephone lines and masses of property of every description. The police and fire services were backed up by the civil defence corps, which included the air raid wardens who were trained in bomb recognition, local fire fighting and helping with rescue work.

Our dilapidated old Orphanage was in good condition during the war years and was taken over by a company of the East Yorkshire Regiment, sent there to guard the docks and port facilities. I can see them now in my mind's eye being marched up Barrack Street under the command of a corporal or lance corporal, rifles at the slope, to change guard at the dock gate entrance. The normal gatemen were either Jacky Cunningham or Mr Grimes. The military were placed at all strategic

Boys' Industrial School, Sunderland.

This magnificent building stood in Prospect Row and was originally built as a Mission to Seamen. Then after several years it became the Boys' Industrial School or the Ragged School, the name used by many East Enders. In the Second World War it became the East End HQ for the Air Raid Precautions. The ARP, as it was known, formed a major part of the whole Civil Defence and my father was head warden there for the early years of the war. The Station Hotel was on its right and George Watts and Todd's shops were to its immediate left, but all long gone today except in the memory of the older generation.

points around the entire docks, a necessary safeguard at the time. With bren gun carriers also on patrol we were well covered for an attack until reinforcements could arrive. The town was also covered by strategically placed anti-aircraft guns which were supplemented by the ships in the port. There were searchlights to seek out the night raiders who came so frequently to our town and to assist the guns in the defensive cover. These guns produced an enormous barrage during the raids and, apart from the noise they made, helped to keep the morale of the people up. It also helped to know we were hitting back with the odd success to act as a boost, such as the plane which crashed in Suffolk Street. I actually saw this dead aircrew in the mortuary as Mrs Watson, who looked after the place, lived in our street.

We got a great boost when the news of the sinking of the *Graf Spee* came through. Three little British cruisers against a powerful pocket battleship. Yippee, it was great news for a lad like me who learned for the first time where the River Plate was, or places like Purnambuco in South America existed, as I marked them up on my war map in my bedroom. I followed every campaign on that map and regret not looking after it, but it had served its purpose and other things were demanding my attention. However, my geography skills were improved tremendously with that map. Educational skills were a different matter as the whole system was thrown out of gear, survival was much more important. We were split up into small groups and sent off here and there in case the school was bombed during class times as direct hits took everything with it. Air raid shelters did not withstand direct hits. We lost hours of schooling during this time yet many of us went on to achieve success in later life, basically through attendance at evening classes after work. However, there were some pluses to witnessing the war as we did.

Seaburn Camp was closed and we missed out on that. Middleton Camp too was denied to us, instead we dug for victory in the school garden which went down like a lead balloon but there was a war on. Posters advising us that 'Careless Talk Cost Lives' filled the billboards, as did 'Dig For Victory'. Carrying your gas mask was compulsory, while sweets became so scarce we almost forgot what they were. An orange? What is that? Bananas? Never heard of them. Rationing dominated everything and no one was overweight I can tell you. Kids today get more sweets in a day than we got in a month and men were dying just to keep us fed. Thousands died in the Merchant Navy and it came very close to home for my family with the death of my namesake.

They say a picture paints a thousand words and this photograph of Pilot Officer James Davies Taylor is worth a thousand words to me. He was cast in the heroic mould, braced by a great determination to become a fighter pilot. He was eventually posted to Coastal Command Strike Wing based at North Coates in Lincolnshire and given one of the most deadly aircraft of the Second World War to fly, the Bristol Beaufighter, which earned itself the title of 'Whispering Death'. Jimmy's main task became the job of sinking enemy shipping all along the European coast, from Cape Finnister in the south to the North Cape of Norway, including the Baltic Sea where Germany carried shiploads of iron ore from Sweden to the North German ports. The Germans designed special anti-aircraft ships armed with a massive array of Ack-Ack guns to protect their convoys. The mighty Beaufighter took them on with four 20mm canons, eight wing-mounted rockets and six .303 machine guns. Flying at mast height, he swooped on these flak ships, battering them into submission. This allowed the torpedo and bomb-equipped Beaufighters to attack the merchant ships much more accurately. Jimmy earned a Distinguished Flying Cross for the skill and determination he showed in knocking out these flak ships. He finished the war in Europe unscathed, before being posted to the Far East where he was eventually shot down and killed. He gave me my first wings when he qualified; took me to Sunday School for the first time when I was three years old; and lived just out of our back in the Barracks. He now lies in a cemetery in Jakarta. A real genuine English hero who like the knights of old proved himself without a shadow of a doubt.

This is a typical German flak ship and it is being attacked by none other than Jimmy Taylor on one of his missions to wipe out enemy shipping along the entire western seaboard of Europe. Our planes were fitted with nose cameras

which recorded every action of the aircraft, in this case a mighty Beaufighter doing what it was good at, knocking out enemy shipping. Jim was a great bloke, full of life and determination which won him the DFC for Valour. But he, like many more old East End lads, paid the full price of war. All I have left are memories of a superb man who gave his all for us.

The lady on the left is the mother of the young man who flew the Beaufighter that attacked enemy shipping. He, like all her three brothers and her husband, all paid the supreme price for their country in its time of need. She is Minnie Taylor who is seen here with her neighbour, Ethel Potts, just behind their homes on the Dock Bank, with stacks of pit props for a backdrop. Both lived in the old Barracks which were then owned by the River Wear Commissioners.

TWILIGHT OF OUR RIVER

After being launched from Laing's in 1984, *Colima* is taken down river by the tugs *Ironsider* (left) and *Holmsider* with two more at the rear. *Colima* was the last ship launched from the Deptford Yard.

The River Wear has seen and experienced many things since she was formed at the end of the last Ice Age, being a familiar companion to the people of Stanhope, Frosterley, Wolsingham, Bishop Auckland, Willington, Durham, Chester-le-Street and Sunderland. However, it is the people of Sunderland who have drawn the greatest benefit from her. Nevertheless she has not given her benefits easily, rather the opposite applies for our ancestors have shed blood, tears and sweat in trying to mould her to their requirements.

Our inland relatives have grazed her water meadows with their fat cattle, while our Roman ancestors bridged her at Willington to carry Dere Street north to Hadrian's Wall. The Queen of English Cathedrals with its protective Castle, lies in a great loop at Durham with the high towering cliffs protecting them in less peaceful ages. However, we at Sunderland have fought to control her in the interest of both local and international trade, spending vast amounts of time, mental and physical energy, plus massive amounts of money in the process.

She became what we made her, while we became dependant upon her as Britain evolved throughout the great upheavals of the Industrial Revolution which saw such dramatic changes to her seaward exit. Today, she is slowly returning to her 16th century state of unpolluted

This photograph was taken at the Fish Quay; the cargo being discharged in bags is anyone's guess. The building built on stilts is the old Robson's Brewery which stood next to the ferryboat landing. We then have Wylam Wharf above that and the old Scotia Engine Works above that. The bridges give a guiding backdrop for easy recognition.

waters, sporting salmon runs and higher fish densities which are very commendable indeed. Her banks are peaceful and calm with hardly any traces of 500 years of marine enterprise by men such as Doxford, Thompson, Laing, Priestman, Bartram, Short, Bloomer, Pickersgill, Pile and many others. She has become serene again as in the days of Bede's boyhood. He no doubt fished from her banks or gathered shell fish from the north or south rocks split asunder by a very difficult little river. A university sits astride this great scholar's boyhood home, one of the greatest seats of learning in the formation of Anglo-Saxon England, who's legacy has been immense in the history of our country.

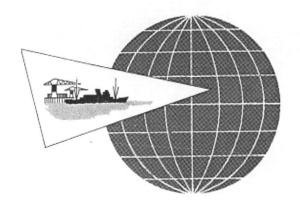

FROM THE WEAR
TO THE WORLD

For nearly two hundred years, ships built in the Thompson-Laing shipyards have carried the trade of the great maritime nations into every port in the world. Today, launched from those same shipyards, vessels of the most modern design, powered by the most advanced type of engines, are helping to maintain and extend the fame of British Shipbuilding craftsmen throughout the world.

An advert for J.L. Thompson's and Laing's Shipyards from the 1950s.

The *Troutbank* under construction at Laing's Shipyard. The ship was launched on 26th April 1979.

But our dirty, polluted, productive river has gone and my mind is left with pictures of a power station seen through the great curving arc of our bridge, belching smoke and steam from a great tall chimney and an immense cooling tower as the water was recycled for the steam turbines which generated the town's electrical power. The smells of Tarry Towsh rope, turps, smoke, soot, tar, along with the clanging of the tramcar tolls, queues for the cinema to see *Gone With The Wind* or the terrible smell of Turley's tripe factory. This was the noise and vast cacophony of sound which encased the whole town from morning until evening as ship after ship was plated and then riveted on the stocks prior to launching. Even the dredger squeaked and screamed as it dredged the bottom of the river to maintain sufficient depth of water for every type of ship which used it. Three short and one long blast of a ship's siren called out 'I want a pilot', and a pilot they got to either see them out or bring them into our river. Ding ding on the tram bell meant go, ding meant please stop and stop it did at the very next stop. Workmen bought Universal Transfers for 2¹/₂ pence which took you from the dock to the town. Then from Union Street you mounted the Ford Estate bus which dropped you off at Doxford before the half past seven buzzer sounded ready to start work. The same ticket, which was usually kept under the peak of your cap, was used for the return journey at 5.20 pm when you finished work. There would be at least 10,000 men employed at both the Doxford Engine Works and the shipyard, and what a crush it was coming out of the Deptford end gate.

I know because I did it as a fifteen-year-old boy, quite an experience, especially in the dark weather of January when I started work in 1945.

My compatriots born in the outlying villages of Murton, Seaham, Hetton, Horden and Washington would almost certainly go down the pit to earn a living. What an experience that must have been for a fourteen-year-old boy, being hustled into the cage and hearing the bell ring. Yet they faced it with unflinching courage, proving that boys too knew how to act like men when the need arose. We never knew at that time how we boys kept the link going between coal and our town, but we did, right to the bitter end of industrial Wearside.

This history of Sunderland has taken us from a sleepy 17th century choked up river, through the whole evolution of the rise and fall of industrial Wearside, back to a sleepy river which is now a quiet backwater. A 10,000 ton ship would be an embarrassment if she was loaded down to the plimsole line and we haven't any tugs to handle her or pilots to bring her in. However, we are not alone in the demise of our port for she has many compatriots throughout the country. She was brilliant in her heyday of that there is no doubt and the battle to bring her to life produced men of outstanding ability. They included: Robert Shout and his piers and brilliant steam dredger; Henry H. Wake who's piers are still standing proud and strong like the men who built them; George Hudson and his financial genius; or the brilliant John Murray, who won and built a magnificent docks from the North Sea in a miracle of marine engineering which has staggered me in its concept. They are an object lesson to the young element of our city of today for they made our river 'A River of Life'.

This is a sight no one on Wearside ever wanted to see, a river, once the greatest shipbuilding river in the world, vacant with not one new ship being built. Twilight was upon us.

The following three photographs, like several in this book, were taken by Ian S. Carr who has been recording North East heritage for five decades. Ian is best known for his railway photography but has also taken many images around Sunderland and the River Wear.

The aft end of the Cross-Channel ferry, *Maid of Orleans*, in Greenwell's Dry Dock in March 1970. Mick Smith, who lived two doors away from our house, drove the crane on the right of the photograph.

The River Wear's last paddle tug, *Eppleton Hall,* lying at the seaward end of the Corporation Quay on 22nd November 1964. It went to work at Seaham the following day. The photographer's father, Thomas Carr, is on the left.

This picture of the old engine sheds was taken near the end of the steam era and shows the maintenance buildings behind the locos in 1965. The granary, on the right, was separated from the railway by a massive stone lined cliff, which arose from the dock level, and a sixty foot wide roadway and rail lines. The lines descended down a steep incline linking the dock with the main rail network. Hundreds of thousands of tons of goods must have been hauled on and off the docks by the engines and crews from these rail sheds.

The Lyons Male Voice Choir based at Hetton takes its name from the Bowes-Lyons family of our late Queen Mother and has been Wearside's representative in many major music festivals, both at home and abroad; winning many top prizes. This photograph was taken in Huddersfield Town Hall at the Northern Championships when the choir finished in second place against some of the best choirs in the North. The author is standing, second on the right of the back row.

The People's History

To receive a catalogue of our latest titles send a large SAE to:

The People's History
Suite 1, Byron House
Seaham Grange Business Park, Seaham
County Durham, SR7 0PY